EUROPE, RUSSIA, AND
THE FUTURE

EUROPE, RUSSIA, AND THE FUTURE

by

G. D. H. COLE

LONDON
VICTOR GOLLANCZ LTD
1941

940·53144 Co2

m59690

PRINTED IN GREAT BRITAIN BY RICHARD CLAY AND COMPANY, LTD. (T.U.),
BUNGAY, SUFFOLK.

PREFACE

I AM well aware that this book has many faults. It is, indeed, to be judged rather as an enlarged pamphlet than as a book. There are many things in it about which I am far from certain, and may quite possibly change my mind. But they are things which, at this moment, I feel need discussing, and discussing without loss of time. I have therefore written quickly, amid many other preoccupations, for fear of missing the right moment for getting them said. If, in the course of saying them, I have given cause for annoyance, I can only plead that what is important at this moment is not polish, but candour, in an attempt to face sincerely and realistically a situation in which it matters immensely what is done, not in months or years, but in the days and weeks that lie just ahead of us. I have never greatly minded making mistakes, provided they help to stimulate thinking. This book is, to a very great extent, an uncompleted process of thinking aloud. The process is uncompleted because, with the world in its present state, we are all of us groping in the dark.

G. D. H. COLE.

Freeland, Hendon.
September, 1941.

CONTENTS

CHAPTER I

THE CHANGING WAR

THE WAR is altogether different since the Nazis have attacked the Soviet Union. For there are now, over the greater part of Europe and perhaps over the whole of it, only two possible endings to the struggle, as far as I can see. One of these possibilities is the general establishment of Nazism as the dominant force in European affairs: the other is the establishment of Socialism. The third alternative that has hitherto seemed possible—a restoration of the old State system still on capitalist foundations—is, I believe, now out of the question over any considerable area as a solution having in it any element of durable success. It may still be possible, as the quite temporary outcome of a war pushed to the point of complete exhaustion on both sides. It may still be foisted on Europe temporarily, if reactionary capitalism comes back to power in the United States, and finds itself in a position to dictate terms to the exhausted combatants. It may still be possible, even short of this, in Great Britain, if Great Britain becomes at the close of an inconclusive war a mere dependency of the United States. But, even so, a peace which left Great Britain in this situation could be no more than a truce between wars. It could not possibly last.

It is the affair of all Socialists both to work with all their might for the overthrow of the Nazis, and to lay plans for the future on the assumption that they will be overthrown. On no other basis is planning even possible. Socialists have, indeed, to work with many non-Socialist elements for the objective of military victory; but they must do this with the knowledge that there is not, in any of the nationalist or

capitalist groups with which they have to collaborate, any
constructive force capable of building up a new order either
within each nation or between the nations. Capitalism, in
all its traditional forms, is dying all over Europe, and
nothing can give it a new lease of life. It is dying, because
it is quite unsuited to the new technical conditions of production, because it has become ineradicably restrictive and
monopolistic and has lost its original character of "private
enterprise", and above all because it no longer really
believes in its own future. Capitalism in Europe can exist
to-day only if it is organised and driven on by a force
external to itself—the force of the Fascist State, with predatory militarism as its primary impulse. For the Europe of
the future, capitalism means Fascism, because Fascism is
the only power capable of keeping capitalism alive.

This does not prevent capitalists in the non-Fascist
countries from joining to-day in the fight against Fascist
domination from abroad. For the various national groups
of capitalists have no wish to be robbed by the Germans.
Even if they prefer Fascism to Socialism, as doubtless most
of them do, they want to impose their own Fascism on their
workers, and not to have a foreign Fascism imposed upon
themselves. Their attitude is liable to change, as it did
largely change in France, when they lose faith in their own
power of independent survival; for then their best hope may
seem to lie in becoming the vassals of their conquerors,
whose aid they can thereafter enlist in repressing the lower
classes of their own countries. But this attitude arises only
when the national capitalists have given up hope of being
able to maintain their own capitalism as an independent
power. Capitalists in many parts of Europe are already
reaching this point; but in Great Britain and, I think, in
Scandinavia most of them have not yet reached it. There
are, moreover, in all countries some capitalists whose feelings of national pride are stronger than their economic
defeatism, and who will therefore continue to oppose

Nazism, at any rate until they become fully convinced that Socialism is the only alternative that remains open.

In Great Britain, reliance on the United States is an enormously important factor in keeping this anti-Nazi capitalism alive. For, as long as Socialism remains a negligible force in America, the main body of British capitalists will continue to rely on the United States to insist on a capitalist restoration in Europe at the end of the war, or at the very least on the preservation of a capitalist Britain. British capitalism is, in addition, greatly encouraged by the attitude of the Labour Party and the Trade Unions, which have so far shown little disposition either to press hard for "war-time Socialism" as an instrument for winning the war, or even to indicate an intention of pressing hard for a Socialist system when the war ends. British capitalism still relies on its ability, with the aid of the United States, successfully to manage Labour so as to keep itself tolerably intact.

These hopes might even be fulfilled, if Great Britain stood alone. They may be fulfilled, for a time, if the war ends inconclusively, with the continent in German hands and Little Britain kept in being as an American Protectorate. But I doubt whether the leaders of British capitalism, if and when they squarely face the problem, can any longer believe in the possibility of restoring capitalism in Europe as a sequel to the destruction of the Nazi power. They must know that they could, at the most, succeed in restoring a series of puppet régimes which would be quite unable to maintain themselves—for it is out of the question that the citizens of the United States would agree to keep a permanent army of occupation in Europe for the defence of such a futile system.

What, then, are the anti-Fascist capitalists thinking? They are, I believe, regarding the latest phase of the war with curiously mingled feelings. On the one hand, they would like the Russians to roll back the German armies and break Hitler's power, or, even better, so to exhaust the Germans, without actually breaking them, as to render both the Soviet Union and Germany impotent for some time to come. But, on the other hand, they have not been able to rid themselves of a long-standing desire to see the Soviet Union collapse, or become so transformed politically as no longer to threaten Europe with invasion by Communist or Socialist ideas. Their pleasantest day-dream is a renascent Czardom defeating both Nazism and Communism at one blow; but they know that this is much more than they can dare to hope.

What I have written so far is but a prelude to the main part of this chapter. For my main purpose in writing is to discuss what Socialists ought to make the foundation of their policy in this new phase of the war. Essentially, the question I have to raise is this. Are the Socialists of Western Europe still thinking of a future in which their several countries will be restored to life as separate States, or are they beginning, now at last, to think in terms of an united Europe?

Free Poland, Free Czechoslovakia, Free France, Free Germany—what do these words convey to Socialists, who are engaged in world war for freedom against the Nazi military machine? Do they mean in the minds of the various Socialist leaders that they are still planning to reinstate these countries as independent Sovereign States, within whose frontiers the old political battles are to be resumed, and progress made, or not made, towards Socialism according to the success, or ill-success, of Social Democratic Parties of the traditional type? If that is what they do mean, they are thinking nonsensical thoughts, without real substance; for it is certain that these countries, so restored to their pre-war ways of government, would fall speedily into even worse confusion than before, and be utterly incapable of finding solutions for the immense problems which will confront all Europe on the morrow of the war.

What then? Ought Socialists to be thinking in terms of federal solutions between neighbouring States? Ought they to set about restoring the old Austro-Hungarian Empire as a Danubian Federation of Republics, or at building up a Balkan Federation by linking together the pre-war States of Jugoslavia, Rumania, Bulgaria and Greece? This notion is no less fantastic than the other. Put back these countries with their independent sovereignties and, even if they agree at the outset to some form of federation among themselves, it will be no time before they are again quarrelling one with another, federal group with federal group, and State with State inside each separate federation.

The idea of nationality as a basis for independent state-hood is obsolete. Economic development, including the development of the economic arts of war, has destroyed it finally. The independence of small States, and indeed of all States save the largest and richest in developed resources, is impracticable now that a mechanised army and air force belonging to a great State can simply sweep aside all the resistance that they can offer. The utmost "independence" any small State can hope for in the future is a false in-dependence, behind which lies the reality of complete domination by a greater neighbour. That, or existence on mere sufferance, or as a buffer between greater neighbours, almost certain to become a battle-ground if those neigh-bours fall out.

Assume the revival of the pre-war European State system, even with federations of the smaller and weaker independent countries. What chance would a federated Danubia have of resisting either a united Germany or a united Russia, were either minded to enslave it—that is, except by enslaving itself to the other? For how much would the military might of federated Balkania count in any future European con-flict? For nothing, as an independent force. Nor, military considerations apart, have such groupings any sufficient basis of economic strength. Can Balkan or Danubian federa-

tion solve the problems of peasant poverty? Yet these are
the basic problems of all Southern and Eastern Europe, and
there will be no stable European order until a solution of
them has been made possible.

I assert the impracticability of putting back the pre-war
State system in Europe, even with federations to bind its
fragments together into larger pieces, not because I under-
value the importance of nationality, but because I am sure
that the first essential for facing the problems of European
reconstruction is to cut asunder in our own minds the
notions of nationality and of independent statehood. There
must be national groupings all over Europe; for nationality
is a real and creative force in the minds of men. But
nationality can no longer, in this twentieth century, provide
a basis for the State. We Europeans can no longer live
under national governments, each asserting its own independent sovereignty, and claiming the last word in all
public affairs. There must be in Europe a territorial
sovereignty very much wider in its jurisdiction than the
territory occupied by any single nation; and to this wider
body must belong, not only the power of peace and war,
and all that goes with it, but also the general control of
economic policy and the last word in all major economic
affairs.

I am not asserting that all Europe must pass, in major
matters of public policy, under a single unitary government. So much I do not profess to know. It may be that
the government of continental Europe will be divided after
the war between two or three great States—an enlarged
Soviet Union in the east and south, and a new West
European State, embracing the countries which have a
more deeply rooted liberal tradition—and possibly a new
Central European State somewhere in between. It may be
that Great Britain will not fall within any of these groups, but
will become, with its self-governing Dominions, part of a
new unit based on the United States as its real centre of

power. But at the most there is no room in the new world of the West for more than these few States, and it may be that there will be found room for no more than one State, stretching from Vladivostock to San Francisco across the span of three continents and an ocean that is no longer a barrier to normal peace-time intercourse.

This I do not pretend to know, and I do not believe anyone can know, at present. A great deal evidently depends on the success of the Soviet Union in resisting the present Nazi onslaught. For, if the Soviet Union can preserve its power intact against the full impact of the aggressors, it is pretty certain that later on the Soviet forces will be in a position to sweep back over a large part of Europe. In that event, is it not most likely that the problems of Poland, and of the Balkans, and of Hungary, will be solved by their inclusion as Soviet Republics within a vastly enlarged State based on the U.S.S.R.? At this prospect, some Social Democrats, I know, will hold up their hands in holy horror. But I, for one, should regard this as a far better solution than any return of these States to their past condition of precarious, poverty-stricken, quarrelsome independent sovereignty, or than any restoration of capitalism in them. I do not like Stalin's methods, and I have been a strong critic of Soviet policy, not merely since the Soviet–German Pact, but long before. But I have never allowed my dislike of much that Stalin has done to blind me to the fact that the U.S.S.R. remains fundamentally Socialist, or that the Soviet form of revolution and of government may be the only one that is capable of sweeping clean the stables of Eastern and Southern Europe, or of solving the basic economic problems of the unhappy peasants of these impoverished States.

Nor do I at all rule out the possibility of a Soviet Germany forming part of this new and greater U.S.S.R. or working in close association with it. Indeed, this might prove to be the best solution, both because German industry and German technical ability would be invaluable assets in the

economic development of these backward parts of Europe,
and Germany ought therefore clearly not to be divorced
from them, and because there is something to be said for the
view that the Germans, or at any rate the Prussians, have
more in common with the East Europeans than they have
with the peoples of Western Europe. I am ready to go
further. I would much sooner see the Soviet Union, even
with its policy unchanged, dominant over *all* Europe, including Great Britain, than see an attempt to restore the
pre-war States to their futile and uncreative independence
and their petty economic nationalism under capitalist
domination. Much better be ruled by Stalin than by the
restrictive and monopolistic cliques which dominate
Western capitalism. Nay more: much better be ruled by
Stalin than by a pack of half-hearted and half-witted Social
Democrats who do not believe in Socialism, but do still
believe in the "independence" of their separate, obsolete
national States. For it would be much better to live within
a system, however barbaric in some of its features, that has
in it some creative force making for the liberation of mankind from class-oppression and primary poverty than to be
thrust back under the dead hand of a decaying capitalism
utterly incapable of fresh, creative effort.

I have not, however, the smallest intention of proposing,
or of working for, the all-European victory of Communism
à la Russe. I am not a Communist, but a West European
liberal (with a small "l") with an intense belief in democratic Socialism. I value intensely the particular kinds of
personal and group freedom which have won considerable
scope under the parliamentary capitalism of Western
Europe; and I passionately want a solution of the European
problem which will leave these values alive and give them
scope to grow. I am keenly aware that Russian Communism, mainly because of the conditions under which it
has grown up, sets little store by these particular kinds of
freedom (though it sets much store by others which in the

eye of history may well seem of even greater account). I know that I should be acutely unhappy in the Soviet Union, or in any all-European extension of it based on the same policy. But I am not under the illusion that my happiness is of any great importance; and I am fully convinced that what matters most is to eradicate the class system, even if the particular liberties by which I personally set most store suffer severe damage in the process. For these liberties, I feel sure, will grow again, within a classless society, in far wider diffusion than is possible under the class system; whereas, if the class system is not eradicated firmly, I feel sure that the civilisation which attempts to preserve it is doomed to fade ignominiously away.

I feel, therefore, that the liberal values of Social Democracy are worth fighting for only if Social Democracy is prepared to fight for them on a basis consistent with the fundamental requirements of the present age. First among these requirements I put the entire abandonment of national sovereignty, and the complete fusion of the "liberal" countries of Europe into a single State. It is for Germans, Austrians and other national groups to decide whether they propose to throw in their lot with an extended Soviet system or with a Western Europe thus united. My assertion is only that there is, and can be, no third alternative compatible with the conditions of successful living in the modern world.

What would be the essential character of this new unified State of Western Europe? It would need to have, as an indispensable minimum, not only the sole control of armed force, but also the general direction of all major economic affairs. It would need to work in terms of a common general economic plan, to accept a common currency, to treat its resources of materials, man-power and accumulated capital as available for concerted use over its entire territory, and to act on the assumption that a common, or at least an equivalent, standard of living should be made available for all its inhabitants. It would have to be, economically, as unified as the Soviet Union, and as fully subject to a common plan.

Are the Social Democrats who constitute the surviving elements of the Labour and Socialist International prepared to face the problems of European reconstruction on this basis? There are two main obstacles to the acceptance of the view which I am putting forward—first, hostility to the Soviet Union, or at any rate to its policy in recent years, and second, national separatism, based partly on nationalistic feelings and partly on the fear that a great, international State may be too huge and clumsy an instrument to express the spirit of democracy.

Take first the case of the Soviet Union. It is easy enough to understand the sensations of fury which visit many Social Democrats at the mention of Stalin's name. They have been, for many years, called every bad name under the sun by the Communists of their own countries; they have watched with feelings of horrified disapproval the successive purges of many of the best known leaders of the Russian Socialist movement; and for the past two years they have been faced, not only with the Soviet–German Pact, but also with the opposition of the Communist Parties in their own countries to the war against Nazism. It is no great wonder if many of them have been ready to believe that there is no great difference between Stalinism and Hitlerism after all, or to rank the Soviet Union among the enemies of Socialism.

Yet this view is, and has been throughout, utterly mistaken. A country does not cease to be Socialist because it follows for a time a radically mistaken policy; nor does a certain similarity of instruments between two régimes necessarily indicate an identity of character or objective. The basic fact is that the Soviet Union remains Socialist in its essential institutions. The land and the factories belong to the people: production is planned not for profit but for use: the class-system has been torn up by the roots. These

are the essentials of Socialism: they are found in the Soviet
Union, and not one of them is to be found in Nazi Germany.
"Totalitarian" the Soviet Union may be; but, if so, there
is more than one kind of totalitarianism, and it is indispensable to keep the kinds apart in our mental classification.

We can now see that what Stalin sought with Hitler in
1939 was no preliminary to a treaty of alliance, but an
assurance of a breathing space. In the Litvinov period the
Soviet Union tried hard to establish a common anti-Nazi
front with the countries of Western Europe—and met with
an entirely discouraging response, because "appeasement",
if necessary at Russia's expense, was then the dominant
tendency in both Great Britain and France. Stalin may
have been wrong—I think he was—to make his pact with
Hitler, but he was certainly not without very large excuse.

Now that Hitler has broken the pact, and launched his
armies against the Soviet Union, it is indispensable for the
Socialists, as well as for the Governments, of the West
European countries to come to terms with the Russians.
Stalin's case against the Western Socialists, put in the fewest
possible words, is that they do not mean business—they are
not really trying to establish Socialism. I believe this charge
to have been valid against pre-war German Social Democracy, against French Socialism, and against the British
Labour Party. I believe it to be still valid against the
British Labour Party; but how far it is still valid against the
shattered continental parties it is hard to say. At any rate
neither British Labour nor what is left of the International
has given any clear sign that it is laying its plans for a
complete victory of Socialism in Europe as well as for a Nazi
defeat.

To be sure, the problem is much more complicated than
the Communists make it out to be. The Communist
technique of revolution, as practised in 1917, was appropriate
to a defeated country in which the old State machine had
fallen to pieces; and it was also deeply affected by the

economic and cultural backwardness of the Russian peoples. It is quite inapplicable to countries whose state machines are in full working order and include considerable elements of political democracy. In Great Britain, for example, it is not worth arguing whether a Communist revolution would or would not be a good thing, because it so plainly could not happen save as a sequel to a collapse of the existing state machine. Such a collapse could come only as a result of military defeat by Germany, and assuredly such a defeat would not lead on to a Communist revolution. The Nazis would see to that, here as in France.

It is, however, true that nowhere in Europe except in Great Britain and Switzerland, and perhaps in parts of Scandinavia, is the established state machine still a going concern. Whatever Government develops in continental Europe after the war will have to be revolutionary Government—unless, indeed, we are to acquiesce in having the exiled Governments put back precariously and held in office by British and American armed force. Neither the Weimar Republic in Germany nor the Third Republic in France can provide any stable foundation for the future governance of these countries. There will have to be a new régime, and it rests upon the Socialists to see to it that it shall be, for as large a part of Europe as possible, a single unified régime rather than a series of professedly independent national States. For we Socialists are, broadly speaking, the only internationalists : we alone have a clear vision of a system transcending national frontiers.

Or have not even we such a vision? Let us frankly admit that most of our followers and many of our leaders have not. It is natural for the ordinary man to prefer to be governed through rulers and officials who speak his own language and share his national prejudices, ways of living and social traditions. For most of us—even of those who see the need— international government is not so much an inspiring ideal as an unwelcome necessity. That makes it indispensable to

think out clearly in our own minds the means of preserving
cultural nationalism, with its appropriate institutions near
to the everyday lives of men, within the broader framework
of the international State. The nations must have their
Parliaments—or Soviets—to voice their common desires:
they must have leaders who speak their language and think
their thoughts; their institutions must be officered by men
and women who speak their language and share the outlook
of the people with whom they have to deal. But all these
national institutions must operate within the framework of
the wider State, in which, until we arrive at a common
language for purposes of international communication,
there is bound to be much confusion of tongues, and not a
little of thought based on differing national backgrounds and
traditions.

We have to face these complications and to overcome them,
because there is no other way either of ensuring the peace
of Europe or of harnessing our collective economic resources
to the great task of abolishing poverty and insecurity among
the peoples. Socialists of all the West European countries
ought already to be meeting and agreeing upon the general
principles for reconciling the need for cultural nationalism
with the requirements of the international State. They
ought already to be establishing contacts with the leaders
of the Soviet Union and trying to break down the barriers
between the rival Socialisms of West and East. If the Soviet
Government and the Polish Government can meet and
discuss the future, and can come to terms, surely the Polish
and Russian Socialists can also meet and settle their
problems in friendly fashion. War is a great solvent of old
animosities, a great engenderer of new situations leading to
new needs.

The two groups of Socialists—Western and Eastern—have
much to learn from friendly interchange. Let me put the
position quite bluntly, even if I give offence to both. We
can help—we of the West—to teach the Russians the liberal

virtues of toleration, freedom of speech and discussion, and freedom to organise for a wide variety of purposes without being brought within the police supervision of the State. What they can teach us can be put much more briefly—determination and the value of a disciplined party devoted completely to the Socialist cause.

CHAPTER II

SOCIALISM AND THE SOVIET UNION

THE WAR, I have said, is altogether different since the Nazis attacked the Soviet Union. This newness has even its amusing features; for there is no harm in being amused even under the impact of the most tragic events. It is amusing to listen to persons who, only a month or two ago, were utterly sure of their rightness in condemning Soviet aggression in Finland and Poland and in the Baltic States, glibly explaining now how right was the strategy which acquired these territories to serve as buffers against the first weight of the German attack. It is amusing to hear persons who were until recently sure that the Soviet Union was the bitterest enemy of Western civilisation now rejoicing at every report of a Soviet military success, and urging that no time be lost in sending all possible aid to the hard-pressed Soviet forces. It is amusing to hear these same persons, who were until quite recently confidently assuring us that Nazism and Communism were fundamentally the same article, now changing their minds about the character of the Nazi–Soviet Pact, and assuring us that Stalin had at the least every excuse for gaining a breathing space while he built up his defences against the ultimately inevitable Nazi attack. Indeed, these erstwhile bitter enemies of the Soviet Union now go in many cases far beyond those of us who were its friends in exculpating the Russian leaders and positively defending the pact as an unavoidable military necessity. It is most amusing of all to force such persons to the point of agreeing that the Pact was the consequence of a British–French refusal to cooperate with the Soviet Union in building up an effective common front for defence against the Nazis, and even that there is substance in the view that the then rulers of Great Britain and France included in their policy of "appeasement" something closely akin to an incitement of Hitler and his legions to march East instead of West.

These *volte-faces* are amusing, despite the gravity of the issues with which they are involved. For my part, I find it quite impossible to go to the length to which many of the erstwhile enemies of the Soviet Union are now prepared to go in justifying the policy of Stalin in his dealings with Nazi Germany. It still seems to me that even if, in view of the attitude of Great Britain and France, the Soviet Union was justified in purchasing a respite by means of a pact with the Nazis, Soviet policy went far beyond this, or beyond what was justifiable, during the ensuing months. It may have been necessary, in all the circumstances, to conclude the pact: it cannot have been necessary to go to the length of publicly representing Great Britain as the aggressor in the war, of supporting Hitler's peace proposals which assumed a Nazi victory as their basis, or of encouraging the Communist Parties in France and Great Britain to play a defeatist part and deliberately to sabotage the war effort in these countries.

There is, however, no need for me to go into these questions in any detail. They have been considered fully in such books as *The Betrayal of the Left* and, more recently, in Victor Gollancz's *Russia and Ourselves*; and, without committing myself to complete agreement with all that is said in these books, I can accept their general analysis of what happened. It seems clear that the Russians either seriously underestimated the military strength of the Nazis or seriously overestimated the power of resistance of the countries of Western Europe. If, indeed, there had been no real danger of a Nazi victory, there would have been, from the Soviet standpoint, much to be said in favour of letting Hitler, Chamberlain and Daladier fight out this struggle in the West, in the hope that each party would so weaken the other as to leave the road open to the conquering forces of Socialism, when the original combatants had alike been exhausted by the conflict. I actually put this point of view strongly, as an explanation of Soviet policy, in a booklet, under the title *War Aims*, which I published in the autumn of 1939. But the case for such a policy disappeared entirely with the collapse of France. It had by then become clear that the relative power of the Nazis was much greater than most people had supposed, that there was a real danger of all Europe being overrun, and that even Great Britain was exposed to an imminent peril of invasion. Under these conditions, there may have been still a case for the Soviet Union to keep out of the war. But there was assuredly no case for the Communist Parties to maintain their opposition, in Great Britain and elsewhere, to the war effort. For by that time the defeat of Hitler had become a plain necessity for the very survival of the Soviet Union as a Socialist power. It was abundantly plain by then, first, that the Nazi and the Soviet systems were not in process of growing together as agencies of world revolution, and that Hitler, if he could complete his victory in the West, would speedily turn his triumphant armies against the Soviet Union. Yet, in face of this essentially new situation, the Communist Party of Great Britain persisted in its opposition to the British war effort, and continued, speciously but quite wrongly, to regard the war as being fundamentally a struggle between rival Imperialisms, in which the working classes and the Socialists in particular were under no obligation to favour, or to second, the victory of either side.

This attitude, whatever excuses can be made for it on the score of British and French duplicity up to the spring of 1940, had become thereafter manifestly inappropriate and wrong. It involved helping Hitler, with the certainty that his victory would be fatal to Socialism and democracy in the West, and, to say the least of it, highly dangerous to the very survival of the Soviet Union. That it was nevertheless persisted in is a remarkable example, not of depravity, but of the sheer irrationality which has pervaded European politics ever since Versailles. Stalin and the Western Communist Parties were not wilfully wicked; but they were extraordinarily and perversely blind. They could not escape from the shade of Chamberlain, even when not only Chamberlain himself, but also the situation which had made his policy possible, had been swept away.

No doubt there were still plenty of faults on the British side. Not only the British War Office and the British Cabinet, but also, almost as much, the British Left underestimated the military power and skill of the Soviet Union. "Of course, the Germans will go through them like butter" was a remark often heard in Labour as well as Tory circles on the morrow of the Nazi onslaught on the Soviet Union. There was a very widespread disposition to believe in Russian inefficiency—a traditional notion—as persisting despite the Revolution and the enormous strides in industrial development made under the Five Year Plans. There was a 'myth' of Russian military and economic inferiority, which was not dispelled until it had been put to the test of actual warfare.

Nor was this all. The very persons who were so quick to change their minds about "our gallant Russian allies" still retained their old hatred of Bolshevism. Ready enough to welcome the respite accorded to them by the transference to the East of the main fronts of war, and by the cessation of serious air bombardments in this country, they remained as hostile as ever to everything the Russians stand for, and as determined to prevent the war from turning into a war for Socialism of any sort. This caused them to suffer from a curiously divided mind. It made them, naturally, more eager than ever to bring the United States into the war, and to bring about a joint formulation of War Aims by Great Britain and the United States on such a basis as would give Western capitalism the best possible chance of survival. But it also tended, more subtly, to make them inclined to accept the diversion of warfare to the East in a spirit of thankful acquiescence, and hardly trouble to consider what could be done, by military activity elsewhere, to relieve the pressure on the Russian front.

The equally irrational antithesis to this attitude is that of the Western Communists, now converted to ardent support of the anti-Fascist war. These new recruits to the war cause regard the entire struggle exclusively from the standpoint of the Soviet Union. They support the war, not because the Nazis are threatening all Western civilisation and every democratic and national liberty, but, from what they say, solely because the Soviet Union is in danger. I share their horror at the thought of the great Socialist constructive work of the past twenty years being demolished by barbaric force. But I am horrified no less at the thought that all the victories won for human decency and for civilised habits of conduct between man and man and between society and society may be lost in a wholesale reversion to barbarism. It is easier to rebuild Socialism than the habit of civilised conduct: the Soviet Union would rise again from the ruins of war more easily than the decencies of human behaviour would be won back if they were once really dethroned over the entire Western hemisphere.

I have to say these things, because not to say them would be dishonest. But I have no wish to dwell upon them. What matters at present is, in the main, not whether Soviet policy from 1939 to 1941 was right or wrong, or how much of the blame for the outbreak of the war rests on Chamberlain and Daladier, but what we are to do now that Hitler has attacked the Soviet Union and both the British and the American Governments find themselves, with whatever misgivings, pledged to give the Soviet Union the fullest possible support. This is the practical question, which makes all previous discussions of the problem of Anglo-Soviet relations and of the attitude of European Social Democrats to Stalinism entirely out of date.

In answering this question, we must take our stand, fundamentally, on the real achievements of the Russian Revolution. Up to 1917, Russia was a despotic empire, ruling tyrannically both over many subject peoples and over the Russians themselves, economically and culturally very backward, with a tiny middle class consisting mainly of officials tied by function to the Czarist autocracy, a very small capitalist class largely under foreign influence and making use largely of foreign technicians, a small but active industrial proletariat, massed in great factories and subjected to very severe repression, and a vast peasant population which was mainly inert in politics and also sharply divided in interest between relatively well-to-do peasant proprietors and a grossly exploited class of poor peasants hardly more than nominally released from serfdom.

As against all this, Russia to-day, whatever the character of its political government, presents economically and in terms of class-structure an utterly different picture. The old upper and middle classes have gone completely; the capitalist class and the foreign capitalist influence over Russian economic development have been entirely removed; the industrial proletariat, greatly reinforced by the growth of Soviet industry, has become the leading class in the country; and the peasants, working under the new collective system, have made great strides forward both in agricultural efficiency and in political and cultural maturity. The entire Soviet economy now rests on a basis of public interest. The profit motive and the motive of class-exploitation have been swept away; and the use of the national resources is planned, from start to finish, on a basis of public service. Common ownership is the rule: private property has become a matter of personal possession for use, instead of an instrument of exploitation. The processes of education have been thoroughly democratised, and educational practice is inspired by a new spirit of public service. National oppression has been ended by the grant of extensive cultural autonomy, above all to the peoples whose traditions differ most from those of the Russians themselves. If we look only at the credit side of what has been done, the achievement of less than a generation appears truly marvellous.

There is, however, a debit account. Some of these great achievements—notably the liquidation of the richer peasants, the *kulaks*—have been brought about with what seems to us a terrible disregard of suffering. In the political sphere, disagreement with the policy approved by the Communist Party has been regarded as unforgivable political crime. Difference of opinion has been allowed only up to the point at which a majority decision has been reached, and thereafter persecuted as treason. The old methods of espionage and delation, characteristic of the Czarist régime, have been taken over and improved into devastatingly efficient instruments for the regulation of political conduct—so much so as to have provided the model for the still more ruthless efficiency of the Nazi Gestapo. Marxism, the greatest critical weapon of the modern intelligence, has been in constant danger of perversion into a dogma—an orthodoxy to which every aspirant to success or influence must subscribe.

These are formidable defects. But they are largely explicable by two things. In the first place, a country by changing its political government and its economic class-structure, however drastically, does not escape from its traditions. It carries on, for evil as well as for good, the deeply rooted characteristics of its social make-up, and can change these only gradually, as the new basic institutions of economic life, of education, and of social equality, have time to produce their effects. A country which has in it large elements of barbarism does not cease at once to be barbarous merely by becoming Socialist. Secondly, we must

never forget that the Soviet Union has been under continuous threat from outside ever since 1917. It would indeed
be possible to trace a close correlation between the advances
and recessions of liberal practice in Russia over these years
and the ebbs and flows of the danger of foreign attack.
Especially has the renewal of a serious danger since the rise
of Hitler been accompanied by a return of more repressive
habits—with a brief 'let up' at the time when it seemed possible that the Western countries would respond to Litvinov's
appeals for a common front of civilised Europe against the
Fascist peril.

It is foolish, bearing these conditions in mind, to fix our
thoughts upon what has been evil in the government of the
Soviet Union, and to forget that none of the evils have
assailed the fundamental character of the Revolution, or
made Russia less a Socialist country than it emerged from
the revolutions of twenty years ago. The essential economic
institutions of Socialism have been not merely maintained,
but immensely strengthened. I know it is often said that a
new system of class-divisions is growing up within Soviet
society—a bureaucracy of officials and technicians lording
it over the common people, and a superior class of industrial
workers claiming primacy over the peasant majority. But
I altogether deny that this is a true picture. No one pretends
that Soviet society is equalitarian in the sense that all men
in it have equal, or nearly equal, incomes. The income differences are wide—too wide; but they correspond accurately
enough to the declared aims of the Revolution at its formative stage. Following Marx's precept, Lenin and his
successors set out to abolish, in the first place, not economic
inequality, but only that part of it which rested on private
ownership of the means of production, leaving in existence
differences of remuneration corresponding to differences in
quality of public service. It may be desirable to advance
much further than this in the direction of equality—indeed,
I am sure it is. But that is no reason for abusing the Russians

B

because they have felt able, so far, to abolish only one source, the most objectionable, of great inequalities of wealth and income, and have not yet been able to advance to the further stage of bringing incomes from work much nearer together than they have been hitherto.

It is quite untrue to suggest that the Russian Revolution is in process of raising up a new class of exploiters against the people. Nor is it better to blame the Russians because they have not yet succeeded in raising the peasant masses up to a level of equality with the workers in industry. The collectivisation of agriculture was in itself a very important step towards this upraising of peasant standards, social as well as economic, and a definite attempt to broaden the political basis of the Soviet Union towards a fuller achievement of democracy. Educational advance, going hand in hand with collectivisation, was a further move towards the realities of democratic control. In these fields, no reasonable person can blame the Soviet Union for not having gone fast enough. It has gone as fast as it possibly could—and much faster than seemed possible when the new system was in its earlier stages.

As for the standards of living, it is often pointed out that the masses in the Soviet Union, including the industrial workers, are very poor by the standards which prevail in the capitalist countries of Western Europe and North America— apart from the Southern States. So they are; but how could they possibly be otherwise? In order to make them appreciably better, the country must first be industrialised on a colossal scale; and the resources of man-power and materials for this process of industrialisation can be afforded only by keeping consumption down while it is going on. The nation must 'save' an abnormally large proportion of its total current income for the purpose of adding to its future income; and if to this need is added that of diverting a further large part of the available productive resources to the building up of adequate military strength in such a

world as ours, small wonder if the people have to go short—
even as the people of Great Britain are going short in consequence of the use of a larger and larger proportion of
their resources for meeting the imperative needs of war.

Socialism is no guarantee of a perfect society. Common
ownership of the means of production and immunity from
anti-social class-divisions based on monopoly ownership can
coexist with grave faults in political and cultural affairs.
They are not even guarantees of democracy, though they
are conditions of its full effectiveness and valuable soil for
its growth. It is silly to pretend that the Soviet Union is
perfect, simply because it is Socialist. But it is even sillier
to pretend that it cannot be really Socialist, because it is
not perfect.

The ruling consideration for us, in this new phase of the
war, must be that the Soviet Union is, by virtue of its basic
economic and cultural institutions, a Socialist country, and
therefore necessarily the principal rallying point for the
forces of Socialism throughout the world. For there is no
other Socialist country; and in the other two countries—
Great Britain and the United States—which are the obstacles to a world victory of Fascism, the capitalist system
of production and the class-structure which accompanies it
still remain powerfully in being. In one of these—the United
States—it is even true that this system and this structure are
almost unchallenged; for American discontent and revolt,
widespread as they are, have not developed into advocacy
of or struggle for any clearly conceived alternative social
order. In Great Britain, with its much older and more
settled economy, they have so developed; but in doing this
they have lost much of their earlier vigour, with the result
that here, too, the capitalist system seems not to be subject
to any insistent challenge from its domestic attackers, but
only to a vast, impersonal peril arising out of its growingly
manifest unfitness to meet the needs of war or of peace.

In these circumstances, there is a natural tendency for the

adherents of British capitalism to seek reinforcement for their own position by the closest possible links between Great Britain and the United States. The more closely they can link the economy of this country to that of America, and the more they can bring America in as a partner not only in the war, but also in the tasks of post-war settlement, the larger appears the chance both of the war being won under capitalism and of the peace taking shape as a restoration of capitalist power in Great Britain and, perhaps, on the continent as well.

There are two obstacles to this consummation of capitalist desires. One is the steady drive which the war itself involves—here, but not in the United States, or at all events not yet in the United States—towards a collective economy running directly under state control and involving not only collective production but also rationing and a collective control over consumption which gradually pares away the superfluities of the richer classes. The other obstacle is the Soviet Union, still far off in the East, and getting further off, in a geographical sense, as the Soviet armies are forced to give ground, but much nearer in the sphere of mind to the peoples of the West since it has become the partner and ally of Great Britain in the war against Nazism.

Some Socialists are still content to rely greatly on the first of these factors, and to pay little or no attention to the second. This is a highly dangerous attitude. It is true enough that the needs of war are pushing Great Britain steadily in the direction of a collective economy. But let us not forget that the same needs have pushed the Germans even further, and had done so even before the outbreak of war. Collectivisation is a most important instrument of Socialism, and one that is indispensable as the basis of economic life in a Socialist society. But it is perfectly possible to have a high degree of collectivism without having with it even an ounce of Socialism. The same instruments of collectivisation can be applied to radically different uses.

They can serve utterly different ends. Indeed, the very increase in the State's power which is coming about as a result of war may be the means—despite the diminution of inequality in consumption which to some extent goes with it— of advancing the prospects, not of Socialism, but of a totalitarian Fascism modelled on that of Germany, but adapted to suit the different temperament and condition of the British people.

This being true, Socialists must look to the second factor fully as much as to the first. It is absurd to suppose that they can make Socialism the basis of the post-war settlement without the help of the Soviet Union. It is absurd to suppose that, with the Americans presumably working hard on the other side, with the weight of the still unbroken governing classes of Great Britain thrown into the same scale, with all the exiled Governments and their capitalist and upper-class backers working in the same cause (for how few of the common people of the devastated countries have been able to escape!), the Socialists of Western Europe can be strong enough to make Socialism the basis of the new European order unless they work with this object in close association and in broad harmony with the U.S.S.R.

This does not mean that Western Socialism has to adopt as its faith the Communism of the Russians. There are ways of thought and living in Western Socialism, belonging to the common cultural tradition of the Western peoples, which make this impossible, as well as undesirable. But it does mean that those Western Socialists who allow these differentiations to become—with whatever excuse—the foundations of a profound antagonism are condemning themselves, and doing their best to commit the movements to which they belong, to mere sterility. They must learn to distinguish between the immense achievements of the Soviet Union in the field of Socialist construction and its faults of political attitude. They must learn to consider without passion the rival claims of Parliament and Soviet as the instruments of social change appropriate to the conditions of their own countries. They must learn to think, no longer in the easy-going terms that serve in periods of very gradual transition, but instead in terms of revolution and of dynamic action capable of transforming rapidly the entire structure of a society, of protecting it firmly against counter-revolutionary relapse, and of imbuing the whole people with a fervour that will lift their powers to higher levels of constructive achievement.

Nagging at the Soviet Union—a favourite pastime of unemployed Socialists—is the worst possible preparation for the tasks of social building which lie ahead of us. We have to set out to build, not the precise Socialist Utopia we should like to see, but the best we can get; and it is of no use to make for ourselves Utopias which ignore the part in the building which the Soviet Union is plainly destined to play. We Socialists are not so strong, or so assured of victory even when Hitler has gone down to defeat, that we can afford to refuse to work together. We *must* work together, or be false to the Socialist cause. And we, the Social Democrats of the West, are even less than the Russians in a position to be nice in our choice of collaborators. They can perhaps, if things go badly, retire far into the interior of their vast country and prepare for a more convenient time: we, if we are beaten now, shall have nowhere to take cover, and no real prospect that our scattered forces can be ever united again.

CHAPTER III

CAPITALISM AND THE NAZIS

THE ADVANCED countries of Western Europe have been living now for some centuries under an economic system which is called ' capitalism '. The essential features of capitalism are that the main instruments of production and exchange are owned and managed by a small section of the community, and that this section employs a much larger section of the people to work for it under contract in return for a wage. The wage-earners own neither the main implements of production nor the goods which they make with their aid; nor have they any independent access either to the land or to markets in which they can sell products of their own.

This is a broad and highly generalised description of the system against which, for well over a century, Socialists have been launching their attacks. But it is essential to bear in mind that no country is, or ever has been, one hundred per cent capitalist. Countries are capitalist to a greater or smaller extent; and they are characterised as 'capitalist' when they are more so than anything else in their leading economic institutions. Even the most 'capitalist' country has in it elements which belong to a different kind of society. For example, there are great landowners' estates in Great Britain, let out to tenant farmers, which are a survival from an earlier feudal economy. Such estates are indeed now to a great extent run as capitalist properties, just as that other feudal survival, the House of Lords, has been partly transformed into a house of industrial and financial interests. But neither the House of Lords nor the Duke of Devonshire's estates are characteristically capitalist institutions.

In countries which are largely agricultural, large-scale capitalist industries and a wage-earning proletariat are often found side by side with a mass of small peasant owners. Where such a peasantry exists, under any system of land tenure, it constitutes a limit to the capitalistic character of the country. Even though the marketing of the peasant's produce passes into capitalist hands, and the peasant is exploited by capitalist usurers, he himself remains outside the categories of capitalism. On the other hand, the existence of great estates, as in East Prussia or Hungary, sets limits to the extent of capitalism in a different way.

Inside countries which are predominantly capitalist there

may exist, not only as survivals of other systems but also as newer creations, large enterprises which rest on a basis different from that of capitalism. Such are the consumers' Cooperative movement in Great Britain and other countries, the agricultural Cooperative movment in Denmark and elsewhere, and the various forms of state and municipal enterprise. Such movements as these may be more or less assimilated to capitalist enterprise. For example, state or Cooperative enterprises may be carried on through autonomous concerns which are not easy to distinguish from ordinary joint-stock companies; or they may be powerful enough to impress something of their own character on the rest of the national economy, as in Denmark. In general, the widespread prevalence of the capitalist form of business, and its almost unchallenged control over the operations of finance and international trade, give it a very great power of determining the limits and methods of working of enterprises based on an alternative principle; and it is accordingly correct for most practical purposes to speak of the entire economy of Europe, except in the Soviet Union, and of the American continent, as capitalist in all its essential characteristics.

Countries are not only more or less capitalistic: they are also capitalistic in different ways. Historically, modern capitalism entrenched itself first in the processes of commerce, spread thence to industry, where it held its firmest seat in the epoch of expansion which followed the great inventions of the eighteenth and early nineteenth centuries, and began thereafter to transfer its empire to the realms of banking and high finance. The first of these phases is connected closely with the rise and fall of what historians call 'Mercantilism', beginning with the establishment of trading monopolies, great and small, clamouring for protection both at home and in their commercial ventures abroad, and passing over in its later stages into 'free trade', in the sense of a trade open to all men of enterprise without need for membership of any privileged company. Adam Smith represents the culmination of this commercial capitalism, at the stage of complete repudiation of monopoly in favour of freedom of enterprise.

The second phase, that of industrial capitalism, takes over this conception of free trade and applies it to industry as well as commerce. It is the phase of keen competition, in both trade and manufacture, accompanying an unparalleled expansion of productive power and an intensive conquest of world markets by the cheap, machine-made products of the countries which were the first to get the mastery of the new techniques. Then, gradually, this phase was replaced by the third, in which financial power assumed an increasingly dominant place. This third phase was marked by a reversion to protectionist practices and also by a rapid growth of manufacturing and trading monopolies, as competitors joined together in great trusts, combines and cartels for the exploitation of the customers.

This change in the tone of capitalism is explained partly by the sheer growth in the scale of operations—a result partly of technical advances requiring larger units of production and partly of the expansion in the size of the market, with corresponding changes in the techniques of selling and of capital investment. But it is also explained in part by a narrowing of the opportunities for expansion as more countries adopted an advanced industrial technique and began not only to supply more of their own needs for manufactured goods and capital equipment, but also to compete much more intensively for shares in the markets which were still open to all comers. Industry became less competitive and more monopolistic inside each country as it became more keenly competitive between the advanced countries. This led on in some industries and branches of trade to a further stage, at which national monopolistic groups of capitalists joined forces to create international monopolies.

Usually, however, this further stage did not carry with it an abandonment of national rivalries between the great

B 2

capitalist groups in the leading countries. Even when these groups joined together internationally to exploit the markets of the world, they continued to fight one another within their international associations, each group seeking the support of its own Government in furtherance of its claims. Most associations of this type were not permanent mergers of interests, but, like the Continental Steel Cartel, terminable bodies: so that there were recurrent clashes of national interests whenever their agreements fell due for renewal. The capitalist groups in the smaller countries were indeed under this system very likely to be brought within the sphere of influence of their greater neighbours; and there were instances, in oil and nickel for example, of international combines which were not made up of clearly defined national groups. But the general tendency of this latest phase of capitalism was not, as often appeared on the surface, towards worldwide unification ignoring national boundaries, but rather towards a grouping of great capitalist interests under the aegis of the great States which were rivals in the race for world economic domination. The phase was, in effect, one of economic imperialism, based on national monopoly.

During the period between the two wars of the twentieth century these monopolistic tendencies were gaining ground at a prodigious rate. The era of competitive cheapness was over, not in all industries, but in respect of most of the raw and semi-manufactured materials which went to the making of the various types of finished goods; and the agricultural producers, too numerous and ill-organised to form monopolies on the model of the great industrial combines, were at a tremendous disadvantage in the business of exchange, and were impelled in one country after another to seek State aid for the organisation of marketing boards, protective systems against imports, and other devices for raising their prices to meet those of the industrial producers. The world market became a dire confusion of competing monopolies, preferential arrangements, quotas, marketing schemes, regulated systems of bilateral exchange, and commercial treaties designed not to develop economic intercourse, but to bend it into unnatural shapes in the interests of this or that protected group. Germany, defeated in 1918, entered into this scramble of monopolists at a serious disadvantage, very short of capital for commercial enterprise, faced with tariff walls of unprecedented height and number, and compelled to expand exports in an attempt to meet claims for reparations as well as for interest on money borrowed from abroad—especially from the United States.

Under these conditions, the German economic system had come, well before the advent of the Nazis, under a large measure of centralised State control; and the world economic depression which began in 1929 and became general by 1931 led to a vast extension of the State's power over the German economy. Industry was largely in the hands of the banks; and the banks, threatened with collapse in the financial crisis of 1931, had to be bolstered up, and largely taken over, by the State. The Nazis did not make the system of centralised State control over the business life of Germany. They found it largely in being, and proceeded to apply it to their own ends.

Doubtless, this State control over business would not have grown up nearly so easily under the tottering Weimar Republic, and would have been much harder to put on a permanent footing, had it not fitted in with certain marked historical characteristics of the German State, and particularly of Prussia, as the predominant partner in the *Reich*. Germany had been a late-comer among the great economic powers of the world; and German capitalism, becoming important at a time when the reign of unregulated competition was already yielding to that of privileged monopoly, found in the feudal, militaristic order of the Prussian hegemony powerful backing for its aspirations, and developed as the ally, and not the enemy, of the older forms of privilege. This tradition was partly discarded under the Weimar Republic, which aimed at assimilation to the institutions of the more democratically organised capitalist States. But the Weimar Republic was never allowed a fair chance and never established itself at all firmly in the minds of the German people. When it was driven, under the duress of the great depression, to centralise vast economic authority in its own hands, it did not know how to use this authority to re-establish prosperity. It became a hander-out of doles to all and sundry—to capitalists and workers alike, because it was unable to find employment for the millions who looked to it for support.

This was Nazism's chance; and the Nazis seized the State machine which Bruening and his predecessors had created against their wills, and proceeded to use it as an instrument of their own aggressive nationalist and imperialist policies. Making war—predatory, imperialist war—their objective from the very outset, they set the unemployed to work at the tasks of war preparation. This was bound to involve a prodigious expense in terms of man-power and capital resources; but the real cost seemed less than it was because until then so much of these resources had been rotting away unused—so that they could be diverted to unproductive tasks without lowering the consumption of the people below the very low levels to which it had been reduced before. The Nazi policy did, however, involve both controlling the character of production and limiting drastically the profits which capitalists could either withdraw from their businesses and spend, or invest in ways which did not further the Nazi war plans.

The capitalists, for their part, or a sufficiently influential body among them, were prepared to accept these limitations on one condition—that the Nazis would keep their workers in order and prevent a Communist revolution. The Nazi conquest of power was in effect based on a treaty of this sort with the leaders of German monopoly capitalism. The

capitalist ownership of industry and business was to remain ;
but the State was to take a heavy toll of the profits, and the
capitalists, with a practically guaranteed market, were to
produce what the State wanted and to sell and invest under
conditions which the State approved. In return, the Nazis
were to break up the workers' organisations, to suppress
Socialism and Trade Unionism, and to keep down wages and
ensure a regular supply of docile labour.

The capitalists who made this treaty with the Nazis
doubtless failed to foresee at all accurately what its effects
would be. They believed that, when the Nazis had done
their dirty work for them, they themselves would be able to
come back to power as unquestioned masters of the State.
They did not reckon with the force underlying the Nazi
will to imperial domination and racial supremacy. No
doubt, *Mein Kampf* appeared to many of them the mere
farrago of nonsense which, from any rational standpoint, it
is ; and they failed to take enough account of the irrational
forces which had been let loose in Germany by prolonged
disaster, or of the strength of feudal militarism in an
economically advanced country which had never fully
accepted the postulates of the commercialism which it
practised. In fact, the Nazis, instead of yielding to the
capitalists when the work of destroying Socialism had been
done, proceeded to strengthen their hold and to make the
capitalists the satellites of the Prussian war machine.

Nevertheless, the treaty held ; and Nazism emerged as a
new form of totalitarian capitalism, or capitalist totalitarianism, which had, from the standpoint of the wealthier
classes, the supreme merit of having crushed the revolution,
even if in doing so it had curtailed the capitalists' power.
No wonder capitalists in other countries began to cast their
eyes at Nazism not with dislike, but rather with a sense that
here was an instrument which they might at any time desire
to use against their own workers, or more directly to check
or break the rising power of the Soviet Union. Of course,

if they decided the time had come to use the weapon of Nazism in their own countries, they would adapt it to fit the requirements of their own national situations and traditions; and in all probability they would not need to make their native imitations nearly so brutal or thoroughgoing as the original. Especially, many of these foreign capitalists dreamed of an adapted Nazism directed not to war-making, but rather to a domestic tranquillity which would leave them free, with low wages and docile labour to help them, to resume their triumphant onslaught on the markets even of a highly protectionist world.

In this mood, many of the leading capitalists of Europe and the United States were very ready to be friends with Hitler, especially when he assured them that all his warlike preparations were directed not against their countries but against the Russian monster which was setting an evil example to the workers throughout the capitalist world. The statesmen who governed in the interests of these capitalists faithfully echoed their qualified approval with offers of 'appeasement' and with incitements to the Nazis to turn eastward in search of spoils to recoup them for their vast expenditure on armaments. Right up to the outbreak of war, a large section of capitalist opinion in Great Britain, in France, in the United States, and in the smaller countries of Europe continued to cherish these illusions, not understanding that the essential driving power behind the Nazis was not capitalism, which was only their instrument, but the spirit of racial superiority expressing itself in unbounded imperialist aggression. Indeed, all too many continued in this way of thinking even after the outbreak of war; and not a few are still of this mind.

In Great Britain, however, and presumably in most of the Western countries which the Nazis have overrun (though not, even now, in France, or, probably, in the Balkans), most of the capitalists have realised that Hitler will not rest content without pillaging them as well as their workers, and that the dream of a treaty with him whereby they keep their wealth and power while he pillages the Russians has no substance behind it. These capitalists are ready to join hands with the workers in order to fight Nazism, because it threatens them. But why, if this is the case in Great Britain, was it not, and is it not, the case also in France? The answer, I think, must be that the French capitalists were and are really afraid of Socialism in France, whereas the British capitalists, though they fear an advance of Bolshevism in Europe, are not, and have not been, seriously afraid of Socialist revolution in Great Britain itself. If they did come to be seriously afraid of this, I wonder whether they would demean themselves very differently from their French analogues.

Perhaps they would, now; for the war has now reached a stage at which any compromise between the Nazis and British capitalism seems very nearly impossible. Hitler has so threatened the British Empire and Great Britain itself that both interested motives and the feeling of patriotism are thoroughly aroused; and the latter is by no means a negligible factor, or to be explained away completely as a manifestation of economic self-interest. That is why it is now possible for British Socialists to press the case for 'War Socialism' much harder than at an earlier stage of the war, without real danger of provoking thereby a mood of defeatism and 'peace at any price' among the wealthier classes. These classes dare not and cannot now give in to Hitler; and accordingly they must in the final resort accept whatever measures are necessary for winning the war, even if these measures take them perforce a long way towards Socialism.

I do not suggest that any large bodies of British capitalists consciously analyse their attitude in precisely this way. But I believe what I have written does give a broadly correct impression of their prevailing mood. Naturally, as I have said earlier, one reaction among them is a very keen desire to strengthen the ties between Great Britain and the United

States, in the hope that this may put obstacles in the way of an advance in the direction of Socialism. Another natural reaction is to try to give 'War Socialism' as much as possible a Fascist twist, by accepting State control, but trying to get the monopoly groups of capitalism accepted as its agents, and also trying to get with it the utmost possible regimentation of the labour force, up to the point at which such regimentation becomes dangerous through fostering underground movements of revolt. As I have said, and shall have to say again, the mechanisms of Socialism and Fascism are in many respects alike: so that the same measures can lead in either direction according to the will that lies behind them. This is the danger inherent in the policy of pressing for 'Socialism Now', as a means to the more effective prosecution of the war. But it is a danger which necessarily attends all advance towards establishing the mechanisms of social control, unless they are accompanied by real advances in the organised power of the Socialist movement.

Broadly, the conclusion of this chapter is that, though capitalism has everywhere an instinctive tendency to turn towards Fascism when it is seriously threatened by Socialism, the peculiar conjuncture of affairs has for the time being greatly lessened this danger in Great Britain, and diverted the impulse largely into a desire to secure the help of the United States, not only in winning the war, but also in giving the peace a satisfyingly capitalist character. What we must now inquire is how far such a peace is possible. How far can European capitalism be restored as a going concern? How far can it be restored at all, except by resort to the very methods which have been tried out in Nazi Germany? Is any capitalism hereafter possible in Europe except a totalitarian State capitalism on the Nazi model, even though it may arise out of a Nazi defeat? Will the quintessential policy of British and American capitalism be first to defeat the Nazis and then to imitate them?

CHAPTER IV

CAN EUROPE GO BACK TO CAPITALISM?

THE VIRTUE of capitalism, in the days when it was actively conquering one part of the world after another, lay in its expansiveness—in the scope which it gave for many sorts of personal initiative, and in the promptitude with which its exponents seized on every new opportunity for the creation of material wealth. Every new invention, every improvement in the arts of navigation and business organisation, promptly found someone, and usually a great many people, eager to exploit it. Capitalism, under these conditions, did increase enormously the total supply of material goods; and there was probably no alternative form of organisation through which the advances of science could have been turned so thoroughly and rapidly into material riches. There were already dreams of a nobler order, under which production would be carried on, not for the private profit of a few, but for the common good of all. But the apostles of this rival creed had no effective plan to put forward, or at any rate none that seemed workable to most of their contemporaries. Fourier's phalansteries, Owen's Villages of Co-operation—were these likely to turn out material goods nearly as fast as the 'dark, satanic mills' of Manchester?

The great argument in favour of capitalism was that, when all was said and done, it did turn out the goods. And the world needed the goods; for population was growing fast, and the spread of democratic notions was making the articulate part of mankind more aware of the evils of primary poverty. It was true enough that the masters of the spreading factory system were guilty of great cruelties; but were not these the price the world had to pay for the new outpouring of riches? It was true that the manufacturers insisted on low wages and long hours as indispensable means to high production, and thus appeared to refute their own claim that the growth of industry was to the benefit of the common man. But the manufacturers kept saying that the flow of cheap goods made possible by unfettered private enterprise must presently, with the aid of cheap imports of food, raise the general standard of life; and, sure enough, after the Hungry Forties and the tardy establishment of free trade in corn, their prophecies began to come true. Standards of living did rise, for nearly all sections of the people; and the rise continued almost without interruption for the rest of the nineteenth century.

There was, in purely material terms, a very strong case for capitalism, despite all the evil that could be said of it, until a better way of organising the forces of production could be found. The Socialists believed they had found such a way; but as long as conditions under capitalism, however bad, seemed still to be getting better, Socialist arguments were unlikely to command any very wide assent. Even the workers, in the mass, set little store by them, as long as they could look forward with fair confidence to further improvements without a change of system. Marx might prophesy proletarian revolution, as the necessary political concomitant of the progressively 'social' character of the productive process. He found followers in plenty; but most even of his followers continued to believe that the capitalist system would last their time, and that it would remain possible for supposedly revolutionary parties of Social Democrats to squeeze more and more concessions out of capitalism by reformist parliamentary and trade union policies.

Thus developed the curious paradox of Socialist Parties all over the continent, or rather in all the advanced countries, combining revolutionary theories and slogans with reformist practical policies which increasingly dominated their real thinking. Revolutionary parties lived on only in holes and corners, or in countries so backward or terroristic as to give no scope for the pursuance of reformist policies. But even while Social Democracy was more and more accommodating its ideas to a progressive capitalism from which concessions could be gained without revolution, the character of capitalism itself was changing. As the markets and the instruments of production became huger, as more countries became industrialised and the centralised power of high finance increased, capitalism ceased to be pre-eminently a system which encouraged diverse initiative and aimed at maximum production, and came to be more and more restrictive and monopolistic. The free market gave place to the regulated market under State protection; competing small businesses grew together into huge combines. There was a scramble to monopolise markets—home markets by tariffs, quotas and the like, colonial markets by the policy of the 'closed empire', foreign markets by political as well as economic pressure. It became easier, in one trade after another, to make high profits by monopoly and low output than by competition to enlarge demand; and the growth of social legislation and collective bargaining actually helped on these monopolistic tendencies by reducing competition in the labour market and making costs more rigid and price-cutting therewith less worth while.

The extent of this change in capitalism was obscured by the rapidity with which the technique of production continued to improve. Even a highly restrictive business system could not avoid, in face of the spate of new inventions and improved methods, turning out in the aggregate an increasing quantity of goods. But whereas capitalism in its earlier phases had, apart from its recurrent periods of crisis, turned out goods up to its maximum productive capacity, the newer capitalism dared not do this, for fear of glutting the market. The consequence was that unemployment, which had been mainly epidemic—an accompaniment of recurring crises—became endemic as well. The crises continued, and the epidemic unemployment with them; but to this was added an inability of capitalism to find work for all willing hands, even at the top of a boom. In effect, underproduction—that is, a total output immensely below what was technically possible—became characteristic of world capitalism in its new, monopolistic forms.

Such a situation was bound to lead to a violent recurrence of the disease of economic nationalism. It set each country to work on attempts to transfer its own economic misfortunes to its neighbours. Indeed, the reactions of economic and political nationalism were disastrously intricate. The political nationalism of the Versailles settlement created countless new instruments of which the economic nationalists could lay hold. The economic nationalists therefore gave full support to political nationalism; and the political nationalists, in return, became the faithful executants of nationalist economic policies. The result was impoverishment all round, and an economic structure in violent conflict with the basic necessities of modern productive technique.

From this folly there can be no turning back to the old progressive capitalism of *laissez-faire*. That form of capitalism was everywhere dead or dying even before the last war. It cannot be revived because its life-principles of open competition and diverse private initiative depended for their existence on technical conditions which have long been superseded in the key industries of mining and semi-manufacture and the production of instrumental goods, and also in most branches of transport and power supply, and in the sphere of business finance. These industries and services have to be based on huge units; and no power on earth can prevent these huge units from following restrictive and monopolistic policies. Indeed, attempts to prevent them are apt to make matters worse, by causing crises of 'under-investment' and destroying that 'business confidence' without which a system dependent on the psychological reactions of business leaders cannot be made to work.

If, then, at the end of this war we attempt to put the capitalist system back, the only form in which we can put it back is that of large-scale combinations with an inherent tendency towards restriction and monopoly. But clearly to put back this sort of capitalism, without correctives, would be so disastrous that it will be attempted only by the wilfully blind. If it is attempted, and the new Europe is built on this foundation, it is safe to prophesy another great war within a generation, and, during the intervening years, a condition of economic chaos very much worse than that which existed between 1918 and 1939.

I feel sure that the more far-sighted European capitalists either realise this already, or will realise it very quickly as they get down to the business of post-war planning. What, then, will they attempt to do? There are, I think, two alternatives open to them, on the assumption that they reject outright any Socialist solution of the problem. One of these alternatives is a system, closely akin in many respects to Fascism, under which the State will become general planner and director of capitalist policies and programmes, and the capitalists will do what the State tells them—on condition that they control the State, and can use it as an instrument for keeping the working classes in order. The other alternative is that the great capitalist groups will link up internationally under the aegis of American capitalism, and will force the various States to carry out their orders and the lesser capitalists to obey them—in effect, a kind of international capitalist feudalism under American leadership.

If the first of these two policies is allowed to establish itself, we shall have in Europe a series of national State capitalisms, continuing and systematising the economic nationalism of the pre-war years. The difference will be that the new State capitalism, following the Nazi lead, will have to take responsibility for the prevention of unemployment within its own frontiers, by enabling the capitalists profitably to set the people to work. The Nazis solved this problem by absorbing the unemployed into tasks of war preparation, and were helped in raising the high taxation needed for this by appeals to patriotism and notions of race superiority and the desire to wipe out the humiliations of defeat. Such a policy, looking to a resumption of aggressive warfare, will be for some time utterly impracticable among the exhausted populations of Europe after the present war. The tasks of peace, and not of war preparation, will have to be the basis of any successful appeal; and, for a time, it will be possible to make an appeal on the score of the need for rebuilding devastated areas and refashioning the economic apparatus of the European countries. But, when the first wave of 'reconstruction' is at an end, what is to happen? The capitalists, small as well as great, will be crying out for remission of the burdens of high taxation; but the State, without high taxation (open, or concealed under the form of inflationary loans), will not be able to find means of keeping the people employed. Capitalism, in its monopolistic sectors, will consent not to be restrictive as long, and only as long, as the State will pay it for all it can produce. As soon as the State stops paying, it will stop producing, and revert to the policy of high profits on a restricted turnover. Let anyone who doubts this study the history of 'New Deal' policies in the United States. Every time President Roosevelt, at the demand of business men for retrenchment, has lowered government spending on public works, these same business men have promptly cut down production, and unemployment has increased. What else was to be expected, or can be expected if a similar policy is attempted in post-war Europe?

The truth is that neither 'New Deal' work-finding nor Nazi work-finding are workable as permanent solutions. The State cannot go on indefinitely with a grossly unbalanced budget, though it can go on much longer than orthodox financiers used to believe possible. The Nazi economy worked only because it was meant to be temporary, and to end in war. The Roosevelt economy could work only as long as the American public were prepared to stand for a continuous piling up of the National Debt.

If, then, post-war Europe tries the Nazi methods of 'national economy', it will end up either in resorting to intensive rearmament to employ the peoples, or in a recurrence of mass-unemployment leading to economic and political collapse. What of the alternative method—international capitalist feudalism based on great trusts and combines under American auspices?

The possibility of this solution depends of course on what happens to America. It will be made much more practicable if there is a swing back in American politics to a Republican Party still dominated by big business, and also a full acceptance by the Americans of the entanglement of their economy with that of Europe, not merely during the war, but after it. The Americans will have to play an immensely important part in feeding and re-equipping Europe after the war; and this will give them a great say in European economic as well as political affairs. If they take the lead in creating great corporations for food supply, for organising the processes of capital investment, for the re-stabilisation of currencies, and for the sharing out of world supplies of raw materials as predicted in the Churchill–Roosevelt 'Atlantic Charter', their influence on the economic structure of the new Europe is bound to be immense. But, even so, a great deal depends on the mood of public opinion in the United States. If the American business barons know that the American people is intent on being quit, as speedily as possible, of political responsibilities in Europe, they will not be in a position to enforce on Europe either political or economic institutions which can be maintained only by continuous American support. They may try to do this; but their constructions will be liable to collapse at any moment if the European peoples tire of being bossed by American capitalists.

This last paragraph has been written on the supposition that American intervention in the post-war affairs of Europe will be in the hands of big business—that is, on the supposition of a swing-over towards big business in the world of American politics. If, on the other hand, American politics swing leftwards, quite different possibilities emerge. For in that event the design behind American intervention may be, not to establish the rule of the great business corporations, but to introduce a system of ordered world trade and exchange on lines fully compatible with the victory of Socialism in Europe. For the bringing about of such an ordered system of exchange, it is not necessary for America to 'go Socialist', in the sense in which we understand Socialism in Europe. It is only necessary for the Americans to set up trading organisations capable of dealing collectively with the State trading agencies of the Soviet Union or of a socialised West European economy. I shall return to this question at a later stage; for the time being, I wish only to point out that American influence on the post-war settlement in Europe *may* work in the direction of an international capitalist feudalism such as I have outlined, but *may*, if Roosevelt's leadership holds, take quite a different turn.

Suppose, however, the solution of capitalist feudalism is tried. What happens? The world is confronted with the power of restrictive monopoly, made nearly universal, and raised to a far higher authority than ever before. Can there be any way of compelling or inducing these great monopolies to abandon their profit-seeking restrictiveness and plan for plenty instead of planning for scarcity and dearness? I can see no such way. No State will be strong enough to curb a monopoly capitalism which transcends all political frontiers; and all the forces which have made capitalism increasingly restrictive will act upon these colossal monopolies with vastly intensified power. The consequence will be unemployment in the industrial areas and, by way of contrast, in agriculture orders to the peasants to curtail their production for the world market—involving a continuance of dire peasant poverty and a mood of angry resentment among peasants and industrial workers alike. And the result?

What save revolution; and with what outcome save the final collapse of a capitalism which has only such barren gifts to offer to the peoples?

Or is there another possible result? Will the international monopolists create for themselves a capitalist Super-State under their own control? Will this Leviathan then proceed to plan world output in the interest of the great monopolists? And, if so, could such a system be planned for plenty, so as to avoid scrambles for markets, and thus reconcile the claims of maximum profit with those of maximum welfare based on maximum production?

This would be indeed a Utopia after the capitalist heart. But who can really believe it possible? It would involve on the part of a body of highly powerful monopolists a complete denial of the habitual policies of monopoly, and therewith a working together in amiable partnership of a number of great corporations each in search of the highest possible profit, and each seeing in the others a rival for the favours of the world's commerce. Only a Super-State of immense and unquestioned power could enforce an orderly plan upon such a junta of monopolists; but *ex hypothesi*, the actual Super-State would be a mere subordinate creation of the monopolists themselves. There is no solution here: only a possibility of a temporary *pax mercatoria*—until the great monopolists fall out among themselves.

In general, then, are we not forced back to the conclusion that capitalism cannot be made to serve as a basis for any secure or lasting European settlement? A return to the old, *laissez-faire* type of capitalism is simply out of the question. A restoration of the pre-1939 type of capitalism, based on restrictive monopolies each claiming the support of its own State for a policy of economic nationalism, will mean general impoverishment, and will be destroyed by unemployment. A quasi-Fascist capitalism, resting on a nationalistic basis and using the State as an instrument for keeping the poor in order and maintaining economic activity by State-subsidised public works, will lead either to renewed war or to collapse under an unbearable burden of debt and popular unrest. An international feudalist capitalism, working through national States which it compels to do its bidding, will break down through inability to find markets for its products, and under stress of the revolt its restrictionist policies will provoke. Finally, an attempt to extend international feudalism from the economic to the political sphere, by way of a capitalist Super-State, will break upon the same rock of the limited market, and will end in war and revolution when the component capitalist groups fall out over the division of the spoils.

What emerges from this analysis is that no capitalist solution of the European problem—that is, no solution which leaves the basic industries in private hands and continues to use private profit as the incentive to production—offers any prospect of permanence, or of escape from war. But it does not of course follow that no such solution will be tried, or even established for a time, with apparent success, over a large part of Europe. To what extent it will be tried, in any of the possible forms, depends mainly on three factors— the strength of the Soviet Union at the end of the war, the political temper in which the United States approaches the problems of European reconstruction, and the strength and clarity of vision among the Socialists of Western Europe.

CHAPTER V

SOCIALIST PLANNING FOR EUROPE

But, if capitalism has no means of solving the economic problems of the new Europe, has Socialism either? Wherein is supposed to lie the advantage of Socialist planners over those who are making their projects for a restoration of the capitalist system? In this, that Socialism can plan for plenty, and can indeed have no other basis for its planning.

For the material needs of mankind are for all practical purposes illimitable : certainly they are far in excess of our present power to satisfy them, even with the fullest employment of all our existing resources and the fullest application of every available technical device. Accordingly, a system which sets out to base production on human need and not on the prospect of profit need fear no glutting of the market and need resort to no monopolistic stratagems for keeping output within the limits set by the danger of exceeding 'effective demand'. A Socialist economy can always set out to produce up to the maximum, because it can promptly use every increase of output as a means of achieving higher standards of life.

I know there are some persons who suffer under a standing delusion that productive power has already reached such a point that all human material desires can be satisfied, if only we use our resources aright. This view, applied to the conditions of the present, is absolute nonsense. Even the most advanced countries have barely reached a level of productive power capable of yielding a satisfactory standard of living to all their inhabitants ; and a much greater part of the world's population lives in countries which are still an immense way from achieving even this. Even if it were possible, despite war devastation, so to organise production and exchange as to give within a few years a decent standard of living to every inhabitant of the more advanced European countries, how long would it take to extend the same advantages to every inhabitant of China and India? Even in Europe, it is a very different matter to produce enough to give every Englishman and every German a tolerable living, and to secure the same result for every Pole, every Yugoslav, or every Rumanian.

The fact that the problem of poverty is not yet in sight of solution for the world as a whole, or even for all Europe, however the forces of production are organised and controlled, greatly strengthens the case for Socialism. It does so, not only on the principle that the less there is the greater is the need to share it out justly, but also because scarcity manifestly calls for a system which is designed to produce as much as possible. In face of widespread poverty, much of it involving positive hunger and privation, it is *wicked* to restrict output; and any system that is based on restriction and monopoly is wicked as well as absurd. The only system that can be rationally defended is one which sets out to raise production to the highest point compatible with the claims of leisure and of satisfactory working conditions for those employed.

The Soviet Union, whatever its shortcomings in other respects, has demonstrated plainly that Socialist planners have no need to be afraid of producing too much, and that Socialist planning is a tremendously effective instrument. Of course, the Soviet standard of living is still low: nothing else is possible in a country still mainly agricultural which has had to industrialise itself in much less than a generation without help from the outside world. Of course, the Soviet standard of living is lower than it would have been if the state of Europe had not compelled the Soviet planners to expend a large fraction of their scanty resources of capital and skilled man-power upon armaments—with results on which we have every reason for congratulating both them and ourselves today. Of course, the immediate standards of consumption might have been raised faster in the early years of Soviet planning if the planners had set aside less for raising it in the future, or, in other words, if they had industrialised less fast. But if they had done this, they would have been much poorer in the long run—to say nothing of the fact that they would have lost the war and been forced to surrender their freedom and to labour as Hitler's slaves. Finally, of course the Russians, in their attempts at planning, have made a great many mistakes, and would have been much better off now if they had not made them. But is it not better to err in attempting to produce than in devising schemes for preventing 'excessive' production, or for paying worthy farmers 'for not raising hogs'?

The faults of Russian planning are beside the point. What has been proved is that even a very backward country, very short of manual, technical and managerial skill, with no help from its neighbours and living under continual threat of attack, can, by planning on Socialist principles, work miracles, and raise itself in only two decades to the level of a great industrial power.

The Soviet Union had, indeed, one great natural advantage. Its territory was vast, highly diversified, and very rich in natural products which had lain almost wholly undeveloped under the preceding régime. It could set out to use these resources and to work them up by methods of mass-production with full freedom to coordinate its plans over its entire territory, without any tariffs or other nationalistic barriers to stand in the way, and with a complete assurance of ample consuming power among its own people. It could pursue *autarkie*, if it had to, without incurring serious economic loss. No small country could possibly occupy a similar position of vantage; for it would be impossible to meet out of home production the very diversified needs of a small population except at a large sacrifice of economic efficiency. Successful planning for plenty requires large areas over which concerted plans can be developed : it may be possible over smaller areas, but the results cannot be expected to be so good.

If, then, Europe needs economic planning for plenty, on lines analogous to those of Soviet planning, it is evident that Europe needs to be economically unified. Successful European planning is inconsistent with the continued division of the continent among a large number of independent States, each intent on pursuing its own peculiar advantage at the expense of the rest. A Europe made up of independent, national Socialist Republics, each retaining its own separate economic policy and trying to enrich its own people without regard for others, might be much better than a capitalist Europe. But it would be quite unable to cure European poverty, or to make any effective provision for the development of Europe's economic resources.

In subsequent chapters I shall be dealing more fully with the requirements of an economic plan for Europe. Here my concern is to stress the need for Socialism as a basis for such a plan. For what force, short of Socialism, is capable of unifying Europe on the principle of planning for maximum production and popular welfare? Socialism, we have seen, can do this because the Socialist criterion of the worthwhileness of production is not profit, but need. No other system can.

Suppose, now, we were setting out to make, on this criterion, an economic plan for Europe. What would be the outstanding problems we should need to solve? I should put foremost among them the problem of peasant poverty in the East and South, and the problem of industrial depression in the more advanced countries of the West. Clearly, the first approximation to a solution of these problems is to provide for an effective and fair exchange of the agricultural surpluses of the East and South for the industrial surpluses of the Western countries.

But, it will be asked, is not this precisely what the Nazis have been trying to do ever since they came to power? It is, and it isn't. Exchanges of industrial for agricultural surpluses they have organised: fair exchanges, emphatically no. They have exploited the peasant countries for their own advantage, giving them few and poor industrial goods in exchange for their agricultural produce. Yet, even so, as I have argued elsewhere in this book, I believe the peasant countries were in 1939 better off on the basis of these unfair exchanges than they were before the Germans came into their markets; for they were so circumstanced as to be better off with a bad market than with no market at all.

In truth, however, this talk about exchange of surpluses is misleading. The peasants of Southern and Eastern Europe have no agricultural surpluses, in any real sense. They could eat all they can produce, and be left crying out hungrily for more. The only sense in which they have a surplus is that they must, in order to keep their land, get cash to pay rent or compensation to past landowners, interest to money-lenders, and money for industrial goods and farm supplies without which they cannot live or produce. The real problem is not to restore this type of trade, which tears the needed food out of the mouths of the peasant and his family, but to raise the level of productivity in these poor and backward countries. This is a matter partly of agricultural education, of provision of capital for land-improvement, of diversification of crops, with the requisite provision for markets, and of stopping the extortions of moneylenders and landowners who tyrannise over the peasant holders. But it is also a matter of removing surplus population from the tiny holdings on which they are crowded, of developing openings for industrial employment, or of reopening the channels of migration, which have been almost closed during the European anarchy. A plan for Europe, in its application to those countries, would be partly a plan for improving the quality of agriculture, partly a plan for finding better markets, partly a plan for developing local industries, and partly a plan for restoring the lost mobility of the peasant populations. But what hope can there be for any such projects, except within the framework of a common plan extending over most of Europe—if not further still?

Indeed, it would have to extend further; for it would be highly unfortunate—though less unfortunate than having no common plan at all—if European planning were to be based on the idea of making Europe as far as possible self-sufficient, and cutting off the trade with other continents in such goods as could be produced in Europe if no regard at all were given to relative costs. For one thing, the entry of Great Britain into any European plan conceived in these terms would be out of the question. It would be plain folly to ruin New Zealand, Australia, Canada, or the Argentine in order to build up a closed European system; and no one in his senses would propose that this should be done. It is to the world's manifest advantage that the great agricultural countries of the New World should continue to exchange their surpluses—which are largely real surpluses—for the industrial products of the older countries; and there is nothing in this at all inconsistent with the requirements of a general European plan. What it does mean is that the solution for the peasant countries of Europe must be sought not only in the expansion of primary agricultural production but also in terms of a diversification of agriculture and of native industrial development. I do not suggest that the problems of peasant Europe will be easy to solve on these, or any other, lines. But the directions in which solutions ought to be sought become plain enough as soon as the difficulties are looked at from a European, instead of a narrowly national, point of view.

The development of the more backward parts of Europe, including their industrial development, is essential to the solution of the problems of the Western countries. For industrialisation in these areas will provide valuable new supplies of materials and semi-manufactures which can be worked up in the factories of the West. So far from spoiling the market for Western industrial products, it will create new markets for them by raising the purchasing power of the poorer peoples and stimulating a diversity of demands which only the industries of the advanced countries can supply.

This language may sound highly reminiscent of the processes of capitalist exchange, as they are explained in orthodox textbooks. It is meant to be so. The writers of these books are setting out, not what does happen under modern capitalist conditions, but what would happen if capitalism were working in a perfectly beneficent way. The aim of Socialist planning is not to ignore the comparative advantages of different areas or different types of production, but on the contrary to base the distribution of industry and agriculture on the very principles which orthodox economists rightly acclaim, but actual capitalist business increasingly fails to follow. If Yugoslavia is suited by nature for the production of certain crops and the development of certain industries, the aim of a Socialist plan should be to take full advantage of this suitability. Full advantage cannot, however, be taken of it when each country is pursuing its own nationalistic policy in economic matters, or when there are formidable obstacles in the way of the movement of either capital or labour across national frontiers.

Nor can full advantage be taken when profit on capital is the sole effective criterion of the worthwhileness of any particular investment—except of course where the State either steps in with some form of subsidy, or itself undertakes investment on a non-profit basis. This does not, however, mean that the considerations now represented by the appeal of the profit-motive are irrelevant. Far from it. How much in terms of labour and real capital it will cost to produce goods in one place rather than another is a very relevant consideration; and so is the elasticity of the demand for one kind of goods as against another. It is also very relevant to know how much production can be cheapened, in real terms, for this or that article by expanding the scale of output, and to what extent any particular kind of production uses up resources which are scarce and of which the supply cannot be easily or quickly increased.

To take full account of such factors as these is of the very essence of Socialist planning. The differences between it and capitalism, in respect of the considerations of which it takes account, are, first, that Socialist planning proceeds on the initial assumption that all the available combinations of productive resources are to be used somehow—up to the point at which there are no usable combinations left—that is, no involuntary unemployment; secondly, that Socialist planning tries, wherever possible, to make its estimates in

C

terms of real costs, rather than of money; and thirdly, that Socialist planning counts not only the costs which fall directly upon the business undertakings concerned, but also the indirect costs—for example, the 'nuisance' cost of smoky chimneys or polluted water, the social costs of unhealthy processes, and the collective costs of providing services in connection with productive developments—such as power-stations, houses and amenities for the factory populations, and so on. This is a kind of costing of which capitalist enterprise seldom takes account; for to the capitalist only those costs which he has to meet are costs in a business sense, and he need not be affected in his policy by any costs which he can compel someone else to pay for him.

Socialist planning, then, involves for Europe the existence both of a planning authority covering a wide area and powerful enough to make its plans effective, and of a body of planning experts trained to think in terms of social costs in the wide sense which I have just outlined. It involves, too, that both the planning authority and its advisers shall approach their problems from an all-European standpoint, reckoning costs and gains in terms not of the advantages or disadvantages of any one country or nation, but of the wider human society which they represent, regarded as a single whole. It must be irrelevant to them whether a development is on this or that side of a particular political frontier: their concern must be to ensure that it is placed where it will best serve the common needs of all.

This attitude is, of course, the very antithesis of that which is taken up by the Nazi planners. The purpose of Nazi planning is to aggrandise Germany and, in accordance with the theory of German racial superiority, to treat all other peoples as instruments to be exploited for the benefit of the superior race. The Germans will develop industrial and agricultural output in non-German countries in accordance with this criterion, and not otherwise, as long as they remain under Nazi rule. But, if they can be set free from the Nazi infatuation, and persuaded to think in terms not of racial superiority, but of European fellowship, there is no people that is capable of bringing a larger contribution than the Germans to the common economic service of Europe.

CHAPTER VI

THE EUROPEAN CHAOS

TURN OVER the pages of any historical atlas, and watch as you turn the changing political face of Europe. The Roman Empire, with its provinces, now expanding the sphere of the *Pax Romana* and now receding before the advance of the 'barbarians' from the North and East. The barbarian kingdoms, settling down to make the new civilisation of the Middle Ages on foundations built by Rome. The Mahometan invasions, sweeping across North Africa up into Spain : the Turks at the gates of Constantinople, and of what was left of Rome's Eastern Empire. The Crusades, the Holy Roman Empire—expressing a conception of Christian unity that was never in fact achieved. The rise of centralised States under growingly powerful monarchs—Nation States in a sense, but almost without a sense of nationality among their peoples ; Counties, Duchies, even Kingdoms, handed to and fro among monarchs by bequest or dynastic marriage or mere conquest without any regard to the collective will of their inhabitants. The development here and there of a more truly national consciousness—in England under the Tudors, in the Netherlands as a protest against being treated merely as a dynastic possession—in both cases an intertwining of the motives of nationalism and religious freedom. The growth of France into a Nation State, absorbing Burgundy and other debatable lands, never fully absorbing Alsace-Lorraine. The emergence of Russia, under Peter the Great, into the European system—a cross between a barbaric eastern empire and a Nation State on the European model. The expansion of Austria-Hungary, a dynastic Empire with no core of nationality to bind it together into a single State. The Catholic monarchy of Spain, unifying itself and casting out the Moorish invaders, making a bid for the dominion of the new world, planting its colonists through Central and Southern America, and then decaying and ceasing to count as more than a pawn in European affairs. The rise of the Dutch, too few to make a political impression corresponding to their commercial greatness. The Reformation, and its sequel in the seventeenth-century wars of religion. French magnificence, and Anglo-French rivalry, in the seventeenth and eighteenth centuries. The great French Revolution, with its democratic challenge to every dynastic and aristocratic régime. The Napoleonic Wars, with Napoleon's armies sweeping over Europe, liberating men from their traditional servitudes but putting a fresh yoke upon their necks by enslaving them to the Emperor's war machine. The prospect of European unification under the Emperor made dim in the retreat from Moscow, and finally eclipsed at Waterloo. The Congresses of the victorious Allies, wondering how much of the old dynastic systems they dared put back; knowing that the messages of democracy and nationalism broadcast by the great Revolution could never be forgotten, laying on foundations of compromise the bricks and mortar of the nineteenth-century system of half-dynastic, half-national States. That system breached, after unsuccessful revolt in Spain and Poland, by the recognition of the new Belgian State and of the 'Liberal Monarchy' in France itself. More Revolutions, predominantly national-democratic but with a proletarian element, in the 'Year of Revolutions', 1848. The crushing of these movements, followed by the unification of Germany, not as a national-democratic State, but as an imperialist power under Prussian leadership. War between Germany and her neighbours—Denmark, Austria-Hungary, France. The French Republic, too weak to stand alone against the Germans' growing power, looking for allies, and veering towards the traditional enemy, Great Britain. Great Britain, more and more wrapped up in trading and imperial concerns outside Europe, standing aloof from Europe, but intent on preserving in Europe a balance of power—which meant, in effect, checking the German advance. The Great War of 1914–1918, ending in German defeat only with the aid of the United States, which began to see itself concerned in preserving the European balance. Following upon that war, a nationalistic settlement, a multiplication of small and economically backward Nation States, an attempt to build up a League of Nations for the maintenance of these States, and of the new *status quo* generally. The firm establishment of the Soviet system in Eastern Europe, as a perpetual challenge to every governing class throughout the world. Nationalist renascence in Germany, under the leadership of an inspired madman assured of his mission to conquer the world for his chosen race : impotence of the League or its member States to check this madman, or to build any system of collective security against him. Surrender after surrender, called 'appeasement'; and then war after all. Pact between the Soviet Union and its hitherto bitterest enemy—the Nazi State, made because Western Capitalism and Soviet Socialism failed to combine their forces in time. Hitler's sweep over Europe, with the Nation States, old and new alike, going down like ninepins before him. The Battle of Britain, the last bulwark in Western Europe. The gradual rallying of the United States to the defence of that bulwark. Suddenly, the flinging of the vast armies of Nazism, despite the Pact, at the Soviet Union. Unity in the struggle enforced upon Hitler's enemies. And next—who knows what?

A history of Europe in a couple of pages, of what use can it be? To remind my readers of Europe's instability over more than two thousand years, of the newness of the political structure which Hitler has smashed in pieces during the past two years, of the mistakenness of thinking of that structure as having any assured permanence, or any sanctity.

.   .   .   .   .

One outstanding result of the last war was a multiplication of the number of States in Europe claiming complete, sovereign independence. Finland, Estonia, Latvia, Lithuania, and the largest part of Poland were carved out of the territories of the Russian Empire. The Dual Monarchy of Austria-Hungary gave place to the separate States of Austria, Hungary, and Czechoslovakia; and other parts of its territories went to the making of Servia into Yugoslavia, to the enlargement of Rumania, and to form a section of Poland. Albania came into existence just before 1914 as an outcome of the Balkan Wars; and soon after 1918 Eire secured virtual independence of Great Britain. As against these changes only Montenegro, of the pre-war States of Europe, disappeared, by absorption into Yugoslavia. Before 1914 there were six Great Powers in Europe: the United Kingdom, Germany, Russia, Austria-Hungary, France and Italy—and fifteen lesser States, not including such little 'principalities' as Monaco and Luxemburg and Andorra. After the last war there were five great Powers—Austria-Hungary having been destroyed—and no fewer than twenty-three lesser States, again excluding the 'tinies' and also the 'Free Cities' of Danzig and Memel.

Of the twenty-one States which existed before 1914, quite a number were of fairly recent origin as independent sovereign societies. Rumania, Serbia, Montenegro, Bulgaria and Greece had been taken during the preceding century from the decaying Turkish Empire. Norway and Sweden, Belgium and Holland, had broken the connections which in the settlement after the Napoleonic Wars had united them in single States. As against this, Germany and Italy had become politically united only in the course of the nineteenth century.

These elementary facts are mentioned here, in order to

emphasise the point that the States of Europe, as they existed in 1939, before Hitler overran most of the continent, had for the most part no long, continuous tradition behind them of sovereign independence as separate States. Of the Great Powers, only Great Britain, France and Russia possessed such a tradition; of the smaller States, only Switzerland, Spain, Portugal, Turkey and Denmark. Other 'nations', such as Germany and Italy, had long-standing national traditions; but not until the nineteenth century were these embodied in unified sovereign States. In other parts of Europe territories included in the greater States had a historic sense of nationality and lost independence—for example, Finland, Bohemia, Poland, Eire and, to a lesser extent, some of the other States set up after 1918. But in many areas there were powerful cross-currents, as the statesmen of Versailles found when they set out to draw the frontiers of the new Europe on a basis of national self-determination. It was not obvious that Czechs, Slovaks and Ruthenes ought to be combined on this principle into a single State, or that Poland ought to include large territories inhabited mainly by Ukrainians and White Russians, or where the lines should be drawn between Hungary and Rumania, or Poland and Lithuania, or Czechoslovakia and Germany, or Poland and Germany. There was, and could be no finally right solution, as long as the problem was envisaged in purely nationalistic terms, and there seemed to be no middle course between complete independence and mere absorption into a neighbouring sovereign State dominated by persons of a different nationality.

In practice, the principle of national self-determination was by no means fully followed, because considerations of strategic strength and economic advantage were also taken into account in deciding where the new frontiers should be placed. But even if the settlement had been purely nationalistic in intention, there could have been no assurance of final rightness, even from this limited point of view.

If Europe had to be parted out among a number of absolutely independent sovereign States, there could be no way of satisfying the populations of territories in which men of different nationalities and traditions were living inextricably mixed up. In a very few cases—in Greece, Bulgaria and Turkey especially—an attempt was made to solve the problem by mass exchange of populations. But such solutions were both very expensive and hardly applicable to communities living at more than a very low peasant standard.

In the light of these facts about the recent past, is there any valid reason for supposing that, at the end of this war, Europe will revert to the precise number of States, or to the same political frontiers, as emerged from the settlement after the last war? Are the States which have been overrun or dismembered since 1939 really likely to resume their old shapes, as if Hitler and the great war which is now being waged had never been? Indeed, ought we to wish to put back these States in their previous form, after our experience of the condition of Europe during the two decades between the wars?

In every case there will no doubt be advocates of a return to the *status quo ante bellum*. Every State that has existed even for a few years brings into existence its own admirers—its politicians and administrators, vested interests, political and economic, that are bound up with its continuance, and even, unless the entire conception of it was outrageous from the start, its disinterested devotees, who see in it the embodiment of a desired national unity. It is hardly to be expected that any of the exiled Governments now domiciled in Great Britain will fail to demand the restoration of the State which it still purports to represent, and, over and above this, there will be many citizens of these States who will readily identify the restoration of their own liberties with the restoration of the States by whose downfall they were lost. Revolutionary movements generated under the stress of foreign conquest will tend to take a strongly nationalistic form; and this nationalism will tend to express itself in a demand for a return to sovereign independence.

It does not at all follow that this attitude is right, however natural it may be. For one lesson of the past two decades, and above all of the past two years, is that small States cannot, under the conditions of the present time, be really independent. In military power they are bound to be nugatory; for it is out of the question for them either to afford the enormously expensive equipment which mechanised armies require, or to build up industries which are capable of sustaining the burden of modern war. But, in a world in which the appeal to force still lies at the back of international relationships, the sovereign State which is utterly unable to defend its frontiers is an anomaly. It can no doubt be argued that the statesmen of Versailles, who set up such States, had also in mind the abandonment of the appeal to force. But their attempt to create a League of Nations for this purpose was fated to break down from the moment when they decided to found the League on a recognition of the entire sovereignty of each of the States which were to make it up.

The sovereign State implies, as part of the very idea of sovereignty, a rejection of obligation to be bound by any higher judgment. It thereby implies its claim to use force in the last resort. But what is to happen if it has no effective force at its command? It can then subsist only on the sufferance, or under the guarantee, of its more powerful neighbours; and the recent history of Europe is enough to show that neither sufferance nor guarantee is a sufficient safeguard when these neighbours fall out, or when any one of them is animated by the spirit of undiluted imperialist aggression.

Perhaps it will be answered that, in spite of this ultimate helplessness against attack, small States have existed and continue to exist in Europe today. Switzerland and Portugal have not been overrun; and Sweden and Finland still maintain a precarious nominal independence. But how much security does any of these States possess; and what hope would any of them have of resisting invasion if the Nazis chose to destroy its nominal freedom? I am not denying that small States can exist, but only that they can, in the world of today, remain in effective possession of the real attributes of sovereign independence.

Of course, the power to defend itself is only one aspect of the truly sovereign State. The conception of sovereignty implies the power of the State to enact what laws it pleases, without any limitations imposed by a greater authority. The sovereign State can bind itself by treaty, and can regard itself as bound, rather loosely, by the precepts of international law. But it can denounce any treaty which it has made, unilaterally and without the consent of the other party; and, as for international law, it can be compelled to obey only with its own consent. The sovereign State is by definition the final judge in its own cause. That is what sovereignty is.

As a part of this sovereignty, the States of Europe, great and small alike, claim absolute and final authority in matters of economic policy. In theory, each State can impose what restrictions it pleases on the course of trade, and pass what laws it pleases regulating the development of its economic resources, the conditions of employment and enterprise, the issue of money and credit, the right of access to its colonies (if it has any), and, in short, every aspect of its economic life. Each State has its own system of taxation, its own monetary laws and regulations, its own national economic policy, which may be more or less liberal or autarchic, planned or unplanned, neighbourly or unneighbourly, at the discretion of its sovereign rulers. In practice, however, this economic independence is, in the case of smaller or weaker States, very greatly circumscribed. They have in practice to relate their currencies to one of the world's leading monetary units: to adapt their trade regulations to fit in with the requirements of the countries on which they are economically most dependent, and to avoid provoking the political intervention of their greater neighbours by pursuing economic policies to which their neighbours may take really vehement objection.

In effect, the small States are, in the last resort, no more sovereign in an economic than in a political sense. But they preserve in both spheres of action all the paraphernalia of absolute independence, and therewith enough real independence of a negative kind to prevent the growth of any effective system of international economic collaboration. They become the unhappy hunting grounds of concession-seekers, searchers after privileged markets, greater States intent on using their economic power to secure the subordination of the economic development of their neighbours to their own national requirements. The little States are drawn within the spheres of influence of the greater, or bandied to and fro between the policies of their more powerful neighbours. Vested interests grow up within them, committed to the service of some larger State, or of its dominant economic groups. Sometimes, the little State may be able to strike good bargains by playing the big ones off one against another. Much more often they get the worst of the deal.

The disastrous consequences of this situation are seen much less in the particular misfortunes of any one State than in the general failure to make the best of the economic opportunities that are open. When each State plays for its own hand, there is no possibility of coherent or rational development of their combined resources. Industrial States find themselves stricken by hunger and unemployment when agricultural States are crying out both for industrial development and for markets for their agricultural produce. Each State, in face of the spreading disaster, is driven, in the absence of any common plan, to seek protection for itself by measures which provoke retaliation and involve worse depression elsewhere. The result is a ridiculous economic parochialism which is much more disastrous for some States than for others, but brings impoverishment in some measure upon all.

Have we any desire or intention, when the present war ends, to revert to this international anarchy in economic affairs? The pre-war situation in Europe was fully as absurd as if each State in the American Union, or each Republic in the Soviet Union, claimed the right to follow a completely independent economic policy of its own, to raise tariffs and embargos against its neighbours' products, to have its own monetary system and banking policy, to regulate the course of investment within its frontiers, to erect its own separate system of commercial and industrial law, to restrict at will migration into and out of its territory, and to use every device open to it for shifting its troubles on to its neighbours, without any regard for the havoc which it would thereby cause. It is perfectly plain that neither the United States nor the Soviet Union could prosper if it were thus broken up into a large number of independent, sovereign jurisdictions, and that the prosperity they have enjoyed is in large measure the consequence of their ability to conduct economic enterprise over wide areas with no artificial barriers in their way. It is no less plain that if Europe is to develop its resources, and to end the reign of primary poverty in its backward areas and endemic unemployment in its more developed centres of industry, there must be economic unification, at least to the extent of throwing down the artificial barriers which have been erected between State and State—barriers which have been both multiplied by the multiplication of frontiers and raised higher and higher in futile efforts to fend off disaster, during the period between the two wars.

If so much is plain, I hope it is plain also that there is no hope of achieving this within a framework of independent national sovereignties. Some Liberal statesmen and economists still continue to argue that all would be well if only the States would of their own accord adopt thorough-going liberal policies—free trade, freedom of migration and capital investment, a completely international monetary and banking system based on gold. But can anyone seriously suppose, in the light of experience, that there is the smallest chance of such a thing happening? There are, in each State, vested interests and economic groups which are determined to prevent it from happening, and much too powerful to be overcome as long as national sovereignty is left in being. In the great States there are formidable interests which stand for policies of economic imperialism and aim, not at liberalising the policies of the smaller States, but at exploiting them as their own spheres of economic influence. In the small States there are petty vested interests standing behind industries which can exist at all only as long as they are protected against the competition of more efficient enterprises elsewhere; and there are half-starved peasants intent on agricultural protection as a means of selling dear at home the produce for which they can find no outlet in external markets. In all States there are financiers who thrive by restriction, and need the continuance of their separate Governments for the successful pursuance of their monopolistic policies. There is no one at all who is in a position to overcome these parochial tendencies—no one able to plan for welfare over an area comparable with the great diversified economic territories of the United States or the Soviet Union.

The consequence is general impoverishment and insecurity, except for the privileged few. So dire are the fruits of Europe's economic atomism that it is quite possible to argue that, in a purely economic sense, unification under the Nazis might be better than no unification at all. I do not suggest that the peoples of Europe are better off to-day, economically, than they were before the Nazis invaded their countries. Far from it; for they are being remorselessly pillaged to satisfy the needs of the German war machine. But I do suggest that the peasants of those countries of

Southern and Eastern Europe which were most subject to German economic penetration before the outbreak of war were perhaps better off with Germany as a market for their produce, even on highly disadvantageous terms, than with no market at all—and this was largely their situation before the Nazis set out to exploit them. The Germans, no doubt, gave them very bad terms of exchange, and compelled them to take in exchange for their produce not what they wanted, but what the German economy could most easily spare. But what did the rest of Europe offer them? Nothing at all: no market for their goods, at any price, and no help in developing their resources or finding an outlet for their redundant populations.

This, as well as the fear among the upper classes in these peasant States of revolutionary uprisings grounded in hunger and despair, explains the ease with which Nazism was able to penetrate their countries both economically and with its political ideas. The States which professed their devotion to the League of Nations and to the ideas of democratic internationalism had been offering these poorer peoples, for twenty years and more, not bread but a stone. The Soviet Union, with its largely agricultural economy, was not in a position to give them much help: nor could it aid politically those who were on its side. The Germans, as soon as they had overcome their own internal depression, were in a position to offer a market; and that, on almost any terms of exchange, was better than nothing.

I say, then, that, *from a purely economic point of view*, it might be better for the backward peasant States of Europe to be dominated by Germany than to be thrust back into the helpless condition in which they were before the German penetration began. But this does not mean that I want the Nazis to dominate them, or that no better solution is possible. On the contrary, the right solution is to be found, not in any form of imperialist domination, but in the working out of a concerted international plan for the common development of the resources of the entire European continent. But no such plan is possible within the limits imposed by the division of Europe into a large number of wholly independent sovereign States.

The plain truth is that, just as the advancing economic techniques of the sixteenth and seventeenth centuries made an end of the closed local economic organisations of medi- aeval Europe, and enforced in one area after another the national unification of the economic system, so to-day the world is passing beyond the limits of national economies, and being compelled to conform to the technical require- ments of a supra-national economic order. Just as the localism of the Middle Ages offered formidable resistance to the growth of economic nationalism, so to-day nationalism is resisting the claims of that wider knowledge and command over natural forces which science has made its own. Vested interests of profit-making monopolists combine with the egoism of local political bosses and the narrowness of men's vision and imaginative capacity to defend obsolete institu- tions and to throw up, as these grow weaker, fresh barriers in the way of applied science and the liberating influence of enlarged ideas. The more obsolete the old institutions become, the more fiercely are they defended; for never is privilege so ruthless as when it is afraid. The new order cannot grow out of the old by a smooth and easy progression; for the old order will not give up without a struggle, and the weapons of the new are at its command, to be turned against all who assail the ancient privileges. Mankind can- not earn its emancipation without paying for it in the birth- pangs of the new creation; and the representatives of the powers that be attend its delivery, not as midwives, but as would-be abortionists of the life to come.

Yet, in this birth of a new world vast in its stature beyond men's historic experience, is there not peril as well as promise? Is not this new age of gigantic mechanical con- trivances and huge-scale organisations too vast for the tiny capacities of ordinary men and women to control? In launching out upon this ocean are we not bidding good-bye to our hopes of democracy? For the only democracy there has been in the world hitherto, in any real sense, has been the democracy of little groups of men who, knowing one another and sharing, upon a small scale, a common life and experience, have learned to work together, with mutual respect and partition of service, upon a few, relatively simple tasks of communal organisation. Sir Ernest Simon wrote, a few years ago, a book in praise of democracy. He found it chiefly, not in London or New York or even Moscow, but in a small Swiss Canton, following a simple agricultural routine, and living remote from the larger complications of advanced European society. The Greek City-States were almost villages, by modern standards of populousness, and Rousseau, whose doctrines lay behind the enthusiasm of revolutionary France, held that real democracy was possible only in small, self-governing communities, of which Geneva was his chosen example. How can men, if they have failed to establish their power to govern themselves over larger areas than these, hope to establish the rule of democracy at a time when the scale of operations made necessary by the advance of physical science far outstrips men's capacity to learn the arts of large-scale political organisation? Are men not destined, under these conditions, to become the prey either of economic monopolists, who can control vast mechanisms precisely because their control is the antithesis of democracy, or of political demagogues who use the mechanised instruments of mass-propaganda for bemusing and spell-binding the peoples, instead of attempting to educate them up to a democratic control over their common affairs?

This indeed will be men's fate, if they suffer themselves to bow down before the colossal image of the modern Leviathan. But if we must not bow the knee before this image, neither can we afford to ignore the reality which it represents. We must learn to control Leviathan, or Leviathan will make us his slaves.

These considerations are highly pertinent to the laying of plans for the new European order. For we must, if we are to find a decent way of living under the technical conditions of our time, at once accept hugeness as the environment of the coming society, and find means of not being drowned in it. The independent, national, sovereign State is useless as an instrument for the effective control of the vast technical and economic forces with which we have to cope ; but, equally, the vast, supra-national authority which alone can plan and develop the new order threatens to become a master too centralised, too bureaucratic, and too unwieldy for ordinary men and women to exert any real influence over its doings, or to invest it with any social purpose corresponding to their own needs or conceptions of what is good.

CHAPTER VII

AN EXCURSUS ON SOCIAL MORALITY

THE WORLD is not arranged to suit man's convenience. There is no 'invisible hand' which ensures that each man, in seeking his own good, as he sees it, shall further the good of all : nor is there any assurance that the diverse ends by which men set store shall be fully compatible one with another. Men have to arrange the world : it is not arranged for them, nor is their path plainly marked out for them beyond a peradventure. They can differ about ends, as well as about means, not only because some men will good more than evil and others evil more than good, but also because different men, and different communities, set store by different things, or at all events put varying valuations upon them. There is no certainty that all good men will come to agree, if only they argue long enough with open minds. There is, in human affairs, no absolutely demonstrable right course to follow among the many combinations that are possible on the basis of a given situation.

Yet there are some things that can be excluded as wrong, even if no one course can be plainly marked out as right. This wrongness is of two kinds. Some ends and some courses of action are ethically wrong, so that only evil or deluded human beings can pursue them. To this category belong the exaltation of war as a thing good in itself or ennobling to participants in it; the will to exercise domination over other peoples, not as a necessary evil, but as an end in itself; the suppression of free speech and freedom of organisation, again not as a necessary evil in a dire emergency, but as a means of ensuring uniformity and ready acquiescence in the ends of the ruling group; the encouragement in men of primitive passions such as hatred or contempt of foreigners in general, or of any particular kind of foreigner; and, last but not least, action based on an attempt to defeat reason, rather than to increase its hold on men's minds.

These are all examples of actions or policies which are morally wrong, and can be justified, if at all, only on the plea that a small dose of one of them is necessary in order to prevent a greater evil—itself an exceedingly dangerous plea. Side by side with these morally wrong actions and policies there are others which are wrong, not because they affront morality, but because they fly in the face of inescapable facts. Thus, it is wrong, but not morally wrong, to struggle for the restoration of *laissez-faire* in the economic world, because *laissez-faire* is plainly incompatible with the conditions of mass-production which modern technology has brought into being—so that, instead of *laissez-faire*, those who struggle for it get for master unregulated Monopoly Capitalism. It is wrong, but not morally wrong, to attempt to bring about a return to the complete and independent State Sovereignty of the separate nations of Europe, because these nominally independent States are bound, under the conditions of modern military and economic technique, to be for the most part incapable of self-defence, and so to become the victims of their greater neighbours, and also because such States are incapable of developing economic policies which will enable the growing forces of production to be effectively used for raising the general standards of life among the peoples. It is man's moral duty to be good : it is further his rational duty to be sensible and not to pursue courses of action which do not harmonise with the objective facts he has to deal with.

I stress this dual character of 'wrong' because a great deal of nonsense has been talked by persons who are determined to resolve the one kind into the other, on the plea of being 'scientific' instead of 'metaphysical'. It is not 'metaphysics', but plain common sense, that every man who is not out of his mind has in him the conceptions of moral right and wrong, however difficult he may sometimes find it to apply them in practice. The very growth of human civilisation is, in one of its aspects, the growth of this consciousness of right and wrong, and of collective sensibleness in applying it. It is true enough that from generation to generation the designations of particular actions as morally right and wrong change, and that between widely differing societies there are very wide differences in the application of the ideas of good and evil. But why not? Such differences are entirely natural, in a world not made for man ready and complete, but subject to his own influence as a shaper of his material and mental environment. What particular things men deem good and evil depends on the type, and on the degree of advancement, of the society they live in. In effect, their complex notions of good and evil at any time and in any place are an important element in their social heritage. They build their notions of good and evil, as they build cities, laws and constitutions, and ways of living in general. The growth of civilisation *is* this process of building, moral as well as material—a building of ideas as well as of brick or stone, a building in which ideas are embodied in brick or stone, and brick or stone made into means of expressing and perpetuating men's ideas of the art of life.

The continuity of a civilisation depends on its success in accumulating from generation to generation its collective experience in the arts of building, both physically and in the minds of its citizens. It is of vital importance that no successful step once taken in building up the idea of good and evil in men's minds shall be retraced. The precise denotation of the things called good will change as circumstances change: the connotations of the words used to express different aspects of goodness will grow wider and deeper. But the ideas behind the words will never, in a continuing civilisation, lose 'weight' or meaning: on the contrary, they will be always 'putting on weight' until each idea has reached the full dimensions of which it is capable. A continuing civilisation will never without disaster wholly discard an idea of good or evil, or suffer it to decay; but equally it will not let it become ossified or lose its capacity for growth and change. The applications of ideas of good and evil must continually change; but this process must be, in a living civilisation, not a series of jumps from one application to another, but a continuous adaptation to changing needs and growing knowledge.

Consider in this light the moral ideas mentioned a page or two ago. The civilisation we live in long ago banished private wars, save in its remoter backwoods; and from the conception of a nation-wide civil order it has been advancing gradually to the conception that all wars between nations are an outrage on human decency. All wars, that is, save wars of defence forced upon men by an 'aggression' which civilised beings have been learning to regard as immoral and wrong absolutely—though I do not suggest that this lesson has yet been at all completely learnt.

Similarly, the common conscience of our developing civilisation has been learning to regard as morally wrong the domination of one people over another—though in this lesson it has advanced less far, and is still apt to regard continuing domination as defensible by prescriptive right, even while it condemns attempts to establish new dominations. Witness the difference in the ordinary educated Englishman's attitude to British rule in India and to Italian rule in Ethiopia. Yet, even in relation to India or the African colonies, public opinion has advanced far enough for it to be necessary for imperialists to assert that subject countries are being ruled for the advantage of their peoples, and not merely by the right of the stronger.

Take again the question of free speech and freedom of organisation. It is not much more than a century (and much less in many countries of Western Europe) since the governing classes ceased, with perfectly easy consciences, to suppress not only all Trade Unions but also all forms of popular political association on which they could lay their hands. The Nazis and their followers have now resumed and systematised these practices; but the common conscience of West European civilisation (from which Nazism is a calamitous throwback) has learnt to condemn them as morally wrong, and to recognise freedom of speech and association as moral goods needed for the expression of the human spirit and for adaptation of social institutions to changing needs and opportunities. These lessons, of course, have not been fully learnt; and the learning of them is so recent that they are not very deeply rooted in the morality of the common man—especially in countries which are comparatively late-comers to Western civilisation. But, up to a point, they have been learnt; and they provide foundations which are indispensable to our civilisation's further growth.

Yet again, man's advance in any civilisation consists largely in his collective success in recognising that difference does not imply antagonism, in realising that men who speak different languages and have different customs are not therefore his enemies, and in substituting curiosity and interest for hatred and contempt as the sentiments which move him in his dealings with 'foreigners'. In many parts of England, even, the word 'foreigner' still means anyone who does not belong by upbringing to the immediate neighbourhood. In Oxford, where I live, certainly a Welshman, and perhaps even a Yorkshireman, is still a 'foreigner' in the minds of many of the local folk. But this perception of difference no longer implies antagonism, or implies it only in an attenuated form which has ceased to be dangerous, and is compatible with friendly relations and fruitful social intercourse. As between 'nationals' whose habits are wider apart, the recognition of community has advanced less far; and for most men there comes a point at which the cross is too wide for antagonism not to hold sway. But Western civilisation is vastly further on towards a recognition of common humanity than it was in the eighteenth century, when the slave trade was the foundation of so many fortunes and only a narrow class had, or could have, any conception of internationalism in its mind.[1]

Lastly, a continuing civilisation implies a growing belief in reasonableness as a social value, and in the encouragement of reasonable conduct as a course morally right. One sign of this is the growth of popular education and, within this growth, the development of a liberalising tendency designed to stimulate the individual to use his rational faculties. Another sign is the increasing toleration, passing over into positive encouragement, of free speech and freedom of association—of which I have spoken already. This does not mean that civilisation involves a belief in the entire rationality of men, even potentially, but only that it does imply a belief that the rational elements in men ought to be encouraged, and their reasoning faculties developed to the

[1] I do not want here to go into the point that this growth of national feeling as against 'the foreigner' was closely associated with the rise of national States, and that mediaeval civilisation in Western Europe was much more international in outlook than the civilisation which followed upon it. This is entirely true, but it is not relevant to the point which I am putting forward in this chapter; and it would lead me too far astray from my argument were I to enlarge upon it now.

fullest possible extent. This is not to say that all the irrational elements in humanity are evil—far from it. But it is to recognise reason as the human quality which, as civilisation advances, ought more and more to exercise a paramount and co-ordinating control.

These values of our civilisation, and others akin to them, are possessions which we are to-day being forced to defend against an attack which, if it succeeds, is bound to wreck our civilisation altogether, and compel the humanity of Western Europe to begin the long and painful task of building decent ways of living all over again. But, it is vital to assert, these gains of civilised living are not, and cannot be, *static* values. We are fighting for the right, not to preserve them as they are, but to develop them in response to changing needs and opportunities. If we try merely to preserve them, they will die upon our hands, ceasing to be values as we cease continually to reinterpret them and enlarge their meaning. We must have after this war a wider conception of all these values, and give to them a wider and deeper practical application, or we shall be well on the way to ceasing to possess them at all, however 'victorious' the outcome of the war may be. For there are no *static* values: everything grows, or it must decay. Nothing stays put in the realm of values, any more than in the realm of science or economic technique.

Moral values are not static; but they are, in their essential nature, cumulative. They continue, at any rate within any developing civilisation, to accumulate fuller and deeper meanings, discarding nothing of their essence as their denotation changes, but growing as fast as civilisation itself grows. By contrast, the rights and wrongs which belong to the realm of commonsense, rather than to that of morality, have no abiding content, and imply no ideal development. They depend on successful adaptations to changing external conditions, and are not only derived from these conditions, but incapable of attaining, like moral values, to an independent vitality of their own. As the conditions change, they change, not by an inner development of meaning, but by a total supersession, sometimes, of one 'right' by another entirely different from it.

To this realm belong the rights and wrongs which are in their essence responses to a technical set-up of forces. It is foolish, and therefore wrong, in a world dominated by the airplane and the wireless, to go on behaving as if one were living in the days of the stage-coach and the postboy on horseback. It is foolish, and therefore wrong, to maintain an attitude to life which ignores the discoveries of Darwin and Mendel and dismisses Freudian psychology as the ravings of a dirty-minded Jew. It is foolish, and therefore wrong, to continue either to believe that the world was created in 4004 B.C., or that its political customs have been fixed once and for all by a combination of nationalist and economic forces which are already of the past.

This realm, of non-moral right and wrong, is a realm at once of necessity and of voluntary choice. Certain ways of behaviour are excluded altogether, or condemned to sterility if they are attempted, because they are fundamentally inconsistent with inescapable facts. Among these, as we shall see later, are many of the ideas of political and economic rightness at present most cherished by professional politicians, academic students, and 'practical' business men. Mankind must walk between the walls of necessity which bound its path on either hand, on penalty of running its head hard and fruitlessly against these walls.

But between the walls is the realm of liberty—of choice between really possible objectives. In choosing among 'possible' courses, men are limited not by the non-moral conditions of their environment, but by their own moral sense, which excludes some solutions, even among those which are not ruled out by environmental conditions of a material sort. But there remain alternatives among which men are free to make choices which raise no clearly defined moral issue, or perhaps no moral issue at all. These choices

may often depend on the relative values attached to different kinds of satisfaction. For example, a society can choose
between working harder in order to have more material
goods, and enjoying more leisure at the price of having
fewer material goods. Overwork beyond a certain point
doubtless begins to raise moral issues—and perhaps idleness
beyond a certain point does so too—but between these points
there is a range of choice which depends on non-moral
considerations, or would do so in a really democratic
society.

This way of putting the case involves a certain over-
simplification. For in reality the realm of morality has no
fixed limits. In any advanced community many issues are
moral issues to some people and not to others. Hunting
animals for sport is an obvious example, and eating them is
another. Some people simply fail to understand what moral
question there can be in matters which cause endless difficulty to others. Now, the social morality of any community
consists of the body of moral notions which finds widespread acceptance among its members, and is not challenged
by any powerful section of its population.[1] It is this social
morality, rather than the moral notions of individual
citizens, that is relevant when we are considering the moral
limits upon social adaptation to changing needs. In a continuing civilisation, changes must be within limits that are
compatible with the elasticity of the current social morality
—not with that morality as it is, but with it as it can become
without destruction of its principle of life. Any change
which goes beyond this will either tear up society by the
roots, or be speedily reversed by a return to enough of the
broken tradition to restore the possibility of continuous
social growth. I believe that the Nazis, having made such a
break in the tradition of social morality, must speedily either

[1] Where one community lives embedded in another, *e.g.*, the Douk-
hobors in Canada, or the black population in the Union of South
Africa, somewhat different considerations arise. But these need not be
discussed here.

destroy German civilisation or be broken themselves. I also
believe that much that has happened in the Soviet Union in
recent years is to be explained as a picking up again of what
is indispensable in the moral traditions of the older Russia—
indispensable, whether it be in the abstract 'good' or 'bad',
because men cannot change their morality very fast without
destroying it.

As civilisation advances, the realm of morality grows
wider. Men's consciousness of moral relationships expands:
they learn to recognise additional duties towards their
neighbours, their fellow-men, the animals, and also inanimate
nature. It becomes immoral to desecrate natural beauty, to
cause unnecessary pain to living creatures, not to uphold
and practise ideas of justice and fellowship over a wider and
wider range of human relationships. The moral oddities
of the few become the accepted ideas of the many, who
come to recognise moral obligations where previously none
were discerned. Tolerance of differences develops, and
begins at length to turn into recognition of differences—
within limits—as a source of positive advantage. Men come
to believe that it takes, not all, but many, sorts to make a
rounded world.

But to a hot pace of change there are, quite apart from
the opposition of ruling classes or of vested interests, really
formidable resistances. These resistances are at bottom of
two kinds, though the two are seldom, if ever, clearly dis-
tinguished. One kind is sheer reluctance to accept changes,
even when they promise plain advantages. The psychological foundation of this reluctance is fear of the unknown—
a fear which is deeply rooted in all men, even the most
adventurous. There are some natural all-round adventurers;
but they are few. There are many more who are adventurous on their own ground, or within the sphere of some special
technique or interest which they have made their own. But
most men are very timid whenever they are 'off their beat'.
Resistance to changes which involve a re-casting of social

habits is therefore formidable, even where morality puts in no word of veto.

But resistance is much stronger when fear of the unknown is reinforced by moral taboo. And, as many taboos which rank as moral have in truth no moral content, but are mere survivals of practices which had once an expediency—a survival value—that has long been obsolete, this stronger resistance may be provoked by changes, even if they belong, in the eyes of reasoning men, to the non-moral realm of 'instrumental' right and wrong, and have no relation to true moral values. It is always the object of opponents of change to invest established institutions with a covering of morality, so as to make their supersession more difficult. To the extent to which this can be done, change can be made harder, even when it is imperatively called for by the needs of a developing material environment.

There is, however, a saving difference. Resistance to changes which are inconsistent with the basic moral traditions of a people persists, even if the changes are made in its despite. It can easily be strong enough to undo, or at any rate to wreck, a revolution. But where the moral element in the resistance is artificial and induced by a dominant class or group in its own interest, it is unlikely to persist strongly after the class or group responsible for cultivating it has been overthrown. This does not cause it to stand less in revolution's way; but it does mean that revolution can very speedily change these elements in the 'morality' of a people without provoking counter-revolution.

It is therefore of the first importance for those who stand for social change to discern the difference between true and false social morality, in order to know in what directions they can safely push change to the limits of their immediate power, and in what others they need to stop short both for fear of the after-effects and because no man in his senses wants to force the pace of change beyond what human nature is fitted to endure. There is, of course, no formal way of dividing social 'morality' sharply into these two elements. Commonsense and personal insight are the final instruments for telling the difference. But it can be said that the distinguishing quality of a 'true' moral idea is its capacity to grow and adapt itself, albeit gradually, to changing situations, without losing its essential character, whereas 'induced' moral ideas have a static quality, an 'ossification', that makes them readily recognisable in any situation which calls for rapidly changing responses—as revolutionary situations invariably do. 'True' moral ideas can bend without breaking: 'induced' moral ideas are stiff, and break readily under any serious strain.

This distinction is highly relevant to the present situation in Europe, where the Nazi Revolution has involved not only a sharp break with the true moral tradition of West European civilisation, but also an attempt swiftly to replace the broken morality with a new quasi-morality which offends at many points the consciences of a large section of the population—at any rate among the older people. Great efforts are being made to indoctrinate the younger generation with this new 'morality'; but 'morality' thus instilled is bound to be stiff and brittle, lacking all plastic quality. It cannot be bent, but it can be broken by military defeat. Nor can there be any doubt that, if it is broken, the older moral tradition, which it has been designed to replace, will be found capable of resuming its influence; for this tradition has not been destroyed but only suppressed.

Of course, the new 'morality' of the Nazis could not have been induced at all unless there had been something in men's minds possessing an affinity to it. It is not a merely artificial construction, but rather an attempt to build upon foundations which lie in the remoter past of mankind—on repressed impulses and primitive urges which were brought back above the ground-level of consciousness by the earthquakes of defeat, post-war humiliation, and severe and prolonged economic depression. Hitler's own mind, as revealed in *Mein Kampf*, is clearly a product of such an earthquake; and he became the *Führer* precisely because a similar convulsion was correspondingly affecting many other minds in Central Europe. It is not necessary, *à la* Vansittart, to attribute Nazism to any peculiar innate iniquity of the German people; for the same under-man is in all of us, ready to be thrown to the surface if our traditional morality is subjected to too severe a strain. It can, however, be agreed, first, that the German nation, or at least the Prussian part of it, had never fully assimilated the moral tradition of long-civilised Western Europe, and, secondly, that the Germans are, more than ourselves, an 'all-or-nothing' people, ever ready to carry the notion 'if I say A, I must say B' to the bitter end of the alphabet.

This latter factor, however, will tend to make the new Nazi 'morality' more brittle, as well as easier to inculcate, than it would be among less pantodogmatic peoples. Even if the Germans, as a people, have never been completely assimilated to the common civilisation of Western Europe, large sections among them have had a very great share in this civilisation, and they possess a great cultural tradition which is essentially part of the common European heritage, especially in the arts. The moment Hitler's military power is broken, these cultural forces will reassert themselves; and Germany, given the right response and reception among her neighbours, will in due course re-enter the European moral system. For this re-entry, however, time will be needed, and the right response is a necessary condition. Another Versailles settlement would utterly destroy the hope of future peace and security. It is one of the lessons of Versailles that it is impossible for long unilaterally to disarm a great nation.

The Russian Revolution, hardly less than the Nazi Revolution in Germany, involved a sharp break in moral tradition. But there was a vital difference. The tradition from which the Russians broke away was *not* the common tradition of West European civilisation, in which they had never more than superficially shared. It was the more than half barbaric tradition of Czardom—a despotic tradition in no wise akin to the 'liberalism' of the West, which was represented only by a thin veneer of Parisian fashion, Berlin technique, and the theoretical philosophising of a small intellectual class. As against Russian barbarism, the Communists stood for the civilising tradition of the West, though even in them it was modified by elements drawn from the barbarism to which it was opposed. Accordingly, the mission of the Russian Revolution was to bring to the oppressed peoples of the Czarist Empire the gift of westernisation. But this, though it remained the fundamental quality of the Revolution, was partly prevented from happening at once by two factors—the very backward condition in morality and ways of living of the huge peasant majority in the Soviet Union, and the antagonism between the Socialist beliefs and practices of the Soviet leaders and the dominant capitalism of the Western countries. Socialism and capitalism were alike Western systems, belonging to the tradition of West European civilisation. But the emergent Socialism of the Soviet Union, being in bitter conflict with the capitalism of the Western Governments, was forced into a partial antagonism to the morality of the West as well.

Marxism, with its attempt to represent morality as merely derivative from the economic forces, and as therefore merely the morality which suited the book of the ruling class, gave unfortunate encouragement to this tendency. It is of course undeniable that in any society many forms of conduct are inculcated as 'moral' because they serve the interests of the established order. But it is a disastrous error to confuse this 'induced' morality with the true morality which forms an essential part of the very texture of civilised living. This error was easy for a mid-nineteenth-century German to make, and easier still for a Russian. But it was nevertheless a disastrous error; and among the Russians many of its consequences have been corrected since the excesses of

the Revolution's early days. I feel sure that the Soviet
leaders are for the most part by now well aware of the
difference between the two kinds of 'morality', and eager
to conserve and develop in their new order the 'true' moral
elements in the Western civilisation which they are seeking
to establish. But they are still confronted with the difficulty
that this 'true' moral tradition is not part of the common
heritage of the Soviet peoples, and has therefore to be
created among them. It cannot be merely released from
bondage by the destruction of Czardom: nor can it be
merely inculcated, as the Nazis are endeavouring to inculcate their 'new morality'. It has to be encouraged to grow
naturally, as a concomitant of the new civilisation which the
Soviet Union is building up by means of industrial development, agricultural improvement, and the spread of social
services and popular education. This natural growth can be
greatly hastened by wise government; but it cannot be forced.

Nor can the Soviet leaders even wish to bring the entire
population of the Soviet Union within the orbit of West
European civilisation, or even of some modification of it
which will incorporate elements drawn from their native
culture. For some of the Soviet peoples, at any rate in Asia
and probably in Europe also, belong to a different moral
and cultural division of the human family. It is a matter of
common agreement that the Soviet Union has been exceedingly successful in handling the difficult problem of 'nationalities'; and it has been markedly more successful in this
field in Asia than in such European areas as the Ukraine.
This is, I think, because it is easier to handle the problem
of nationality when it is a question of large differences,
involving a radical approach, than when the nationalities
whose autonomy is at issue are close together in general
culture and moral tradition, so that the problem tends to
assume an exclusively political, rather than a cultural, form.
The Mahometan and other un-Christian peoples of Asiatic
Russia can be endowed with a cultural autonomy which satis-

fies their national aspirations without raising the question of nationalism in a political sense. But Ukrainian nationalism, to the extent to which it exists at all, is a political and not a cultural movement, and its claims cannot be satisfied without breaking the essential unity of the Soviet system.

In a later chapter I shall be discussing this question of nationality as it arises in Western Europe. Here my point is only that the Soviet Union furnishes a remarkable example of a strong political unit which is not based throughout on a common culture or a common moral tradition, so that it cannot in any event become completely absorbed in any pan-European civilisation based upon such a culture or such a tradition. It must either break asunder, between East and West, or, as seems more likely, remain united and serve as a bridge, or an interpreter, between the cultures of East and West. If it can thus interpret each of the great culture systems between which it lies to the other, that surely offers to the future the best possible hope of a durable peace, not merely between the nations of Europe, but over all the world.

Meantime, the task immediately before the Soviet Union and what is left erect of the West European family of nations is the utter destruction of the false morality on which the Nazis have built their power. For this task there must be not merely military and diplomatic co-operation between the Soviet Government and the British Government as representing Free Europe, but also social cooperation between the British and Soviet peoples. West Europeans, and above all others West European Socialists, must throw off their past antagonism to the Soviet leadership, not recanting the criticisms they have made—for any such recantation would be necessarily insincere—but recognising their irrelevance in the present world situation, and as far as possible putting them right out of their minds. Can it be doubted for a moment that close collaboration and exchange of ideas will be good for both parties to the exchange? Can it be doubted that comradeship in arms and thereafter in world reconstruction between the Soviet Union and the progressive elements in Western Europe will do a great deal to strengthen the forces which are leading the Soviet peoples towards an acceptance of the basic 'true' morality of Western civilisation—of the values of free speech, freedom of association, toleration leading to the ready acceptance of differences, and of kindness and clemency in the daily relations of living? Or can it be doubted that the West will learn from the Soviet Union the immense release of productive and social energy which is made possible by common control of resources, by the abolition of class-parasitism, and by the unification of effort in pursuance of a common plan for the furtherance of human well-being? Or, again, that Western Socialists in particular can learn from the Soviet Union the value of courage and determination, made the guiding principles of a closely knit party devoted without qualification to the Socialist cause?

CHAPTER VIII

NATIONALISM AND THE ECONOMIC ORDER

NATIONALITY IS, by the common consent of those who have made the attempt, exceedingly difficult to define. The question 'How many nations are there in Europe?' is simply unanswerable, because nationality is a matter not of absolute being or not being, but also of feeling or not feeling. It does not imply, though the sense of it may be strengthened by, a community of blood: it can exist, though not without frictions, in the absence of a common language; and it admits of varying degrees of intensity. It is possible for a collection of persons to be more or less a nation; and it is also possible for a group, lying between two more clearly defined peoples, to be quite uncertain which way its national allegiance lies. Nor is nationality a fixed concept in time: national consciousness can wax and wane, die out alto-

D

gether, or be recreated when it has seemed for a long time to have lost all its force.

These uncertainties do not, however, mean that nationality is unimportant. Quite the contrary. It is, among the majority of Europeans, an exceedingly powerful sentiment— one which moves the ordinary man to deeds of enthusiasm and sacrifice more readily than any other social or political concept. It is not so continuous a motive as that of economic self-interest; but this is not because it is weaker, but rather because the occasions which evoke it as a stimulus to action are, in modern societies, fewer and more intermittent. It is, I think, all the more powerful when it is evoked because it is not, like the economic motive, being continually practised upon small things. For it is in response to rare calls, and not to everyday stimuli, that men show their capacity for heroic doings.

Powerful as the sentiment of nationality is, its predominance as an inducement to heroism is relatively modern. Only during the nineteenth century did it become widely diffused among the main body of the peoples. An Englishman of the days of Nelson resisted the press-gang without any sense of behaving unpatriotically; and no one expected the peasants of pre-revolutionary France to be moved by a passion for serving the fatherland. It has often been said that, though the Nation State came in with the Renaissance and the Reformation, the spirit of national patriotism began, over most of Europe, only with the French Revolution of 1789. The watchwords of that revolution were 'Liberty, Equality, Fraternity'; but these words came, as a consequence of it, to be interpreted practically in nationalistic terms.

The rise of the Nation State obviously corresponded closely to economic needs. It was indispensable for economic security and progress that there should be laws uniformly administered over wide territories, national markets liberated from the restrictions of local tolls and monopolies, large-scale authorities to foster the growth of trade and enterprise in distant regions, improved means of communication across wide countrysides, and a host of other developments which required unified administration over the largest manageable areas. These needs did not by themselves call the National State into being; but they caused those who were aware of them to take the side of the monarchs who were seeking to consolidate their hold over great bodies of subjects, and thus ensured the success of the State builders' plans.

But this process of building Nation States did not connote any widespread growth of the sentiment of nationality. The enthusiasms which entered into the wars of the seventeenth century were religious rather than national. Where national sentiment existed at all, it was mainly an aristocratic and not a popular passion. It needed the conception of democracy —of States as belonging to their peoples rather than to their kings or to a ruling oligarchy—to give national sentiment a lodging in the minds of the common run of citizens.

As the spirit of democracy was aroused, it naturally sought first of all to make conquest of the Nation States which were by then the established units of government. In each country, those who struggled to make their State democratic and their own came, in proportion to their success or even out of proportion to it, to attach to the Nation State their collective sentiment for democracy; and out of this marriage the sentiment of national patriotism as a popular passion was born. When it had been born two further consequences followed. Aristocrats sought to detach the sentiment of patriotism from the democratic sentiment which had inspired it, and to convert it into an instrument of the Nation State in its undemocratic form. This attempt is visible in the history of Hegelianism as a political theory, and in the record of many Nationalist Parties—for example, those of Germany and Italy. At the same time, there were many States in which it was very difficult for a common democratic sentiment of nationality to be aroused, because they were made up of subjects not only speaking different languages, but also living at widely different levels of culture, practising different religions, and having little in common beyond subjection to a single ruler. In such countries, nationalism developed on the one hand as the sentiment of a 'superior' national group which claimed the right to shape the State to suit its own convenience, and on the other as a revolt of the 'inferior' groups, which acquired, and subsequently rationalised under intellectual leadership, nationalist sentiments of their own. These latter sentiments, in the circumstances of the time, inevitably took shape in political nationalist movements aiming at the creation of new, separate Nation States, or, at the very least, autonomous national governments within a wider federal grouping.

Thus, in general, the Nation State arose first, and the sentiment of nationality thereafter became attached to it. But among subjected peoples the sentiment of nationality arose by way of reaction from the nationalism of the ruling peoples, and shaped itself as a desire to create new Nation States. In both cases the ideas of nationality and of statehood became very closely linked together in men's minds. It seemed as if only by creating or keeping for themselves a separate Nation State could men hope to have the means of satisfying their common national desires.

The Nation State, from the time of its birth right up to its full development in the course of the nineteenth century, was on the whole a liberating influence in the economic field. It had, indeed, increasingly manifest disadvantages as the markets of the world became increasingly international and as the interdependence of one country and another in economic matters grew greater. But it had for the merchants and industrialists the immense advantage of giving them an assured basis of operations governed firmly by a law which met their principal needs, and in addition a treaty-making body which could with a fair degree of success protect them in their dealings across State frontiers. As trade and industry were predominantly a matter of competitive private enterprise, what the traders and industrialists chiefly wanted was the effective operation of law, national and international, on principles consistent with their needs and interests. This the system of Nation States gave then to a thoroughly satisfying extent; and accordingly the mercantile interests, despite the internationalism of trade, were in general strong upholders of the Nation State and of the sentiment of nationality as attaching to it.

Only towards the end of the nineteenth century, and then not everywhere, did the possibilities of a serious clash between the limits of Nation States and the requirements of the economic order begin to appear. The first clear sign of this clash was the raising of protective tariff walls designed to limit international trade in the interests of national production. Each National State, or rather its rulers, desired to be as powerful as possible; and each group of traders or producers within it saw a prospect of securing differential advantages for itself if it could get the State's support. In one country after another, the rulers and the industrialists carried through a 'deal'—the rulers desiring particular forms of home economic development as a means to national power and the industrialists seeing prospects of better profits in a monopolistic home market than in worldwide free competition with the industrialists of other countries. With this development went also the growth of economic imperialism —the attempt by States to promote both wealth and national glory by appropriating less advanced countries, which could be made valuable either as closed or preferential markets or as exclusive sources of raw materials, or as fields for profitable investment and 'honourable' employment for the surplus children of the ruling classes.

This type of imperialism was not, of course, new in the latter part of the nineteenth century—witness India; but it received at that time a greatly extended application, above all in the rapid partition of the African continent after 1880.

With this process went a grafting on of imperialist to national sentiment, accompanied by a profound modification in its character. There had been from the first an imperialist element in the nationalism of those peoples who ruled over subject groups within their State territories—for example, Russians, Hungarians, Germans, and also of course the British peoples. But the new imperialism was different from this, because it began to envisage the world in terms of a few Empires, dominated by chosen nations with a mission of 'civilisation'—and economic exploitation—akin to that of the Roman Empire in the ancient world.

From that time Nationalism and Imperialism were involved in curiously complicated relationships. Nationalism existed as the enemy of Imperialism among subject peoples at all stages of civilisation save the very lowest; and it was notable that the less advanced the people the more its nationalist movement usually stood for the claims of a privileged order within it (*e.g.* Arab landowners, Indian millowners, Slovakian landlords and church dignitaries). At the other extreme, among ruling peoples Nationalism and Imperialism tended to appear as allies, and even to fuse, up to a point, into a mixed sentiment. Finally, in Nation States which had no dependent empires Nationalism existed as a sentiment attached primarily to the idea of the separateness and independence of the State, though in States of mixed language and culture there were sometimes secondary influences pulling different ways towards the Nationalisms of their greater neighbours (*e.g.* in Belgium).

In all these varied forms, Nationalism has come to be closely associated with the idea of political independence. Each group which looks upon itself as a nation wants to have a State of its own, partly out of a rational desire to satisfy its collective aspirations, preserve and develop its common culture, and be able to have its public affairs administered in its own language and by officials who share its collective peculiarities and outlook, but also partly because statehood has come to be regarded as the hallmark of national success. Each group which has a State wants its State to be expressive of its national character, and tends to seek the suppression within its borders of any rival expression of nationality, both as a potential source of weakness and disaffection and as inconsistent with the essential character of the Nation State. In all Western Europe Switzerland stands alone as the example of a Nation State based on equality among a number of peoples speaking different languages, practising different religious observances, and possessing strong affinities to three larger neighbouring States. Every other 'mixed' State is troubled, in greater or smaller degree, by malcontent nationalist movements among its linguistic, religious, or racial minorities.

Nationalism pressed to these lengths could never have prevailed without coming into conflict with the basic economic needs of the peoples. But the nationalism of the larger national groups was not, until quite recently, open to serious objection on this score. On the contrary, it was on the whole a unifying force, facilitating more than it hindered higher production and the exchange of goods over larger areas. Most of the smaller groups whose national separateness would have been at any time an economic nuisance did not attain to independent statehood until the Peace-Settlements of 1919 and 1920 set up in Europe a number of new States, made out of fragments of the old Austro-Hungarian and Russian Empires. Thus, one result of Versailles and of the other treaties imposed after the last war was to aggravate very greatly the discrepancy between political frontiers and economic needs, by actually breaking up what had been single economic systems into a number of separate fragments and delineating new frontiers with the scantiest regard to the complex structures of production and exchange. The consequent disturbance of economic balance was one powerful factor driving the greater States towards attempts at economic self-sufficiency, or at least towards the re-creation within their frontiers of industries which they had lost by the peace, or towards the creation of industries which they deemed essential to their security in the event of war. In the extreme case, it led them towards war itself, as a means of achieving *autarkie* by bringing 'complementary' countries under their control.

The entire period between the two wars was one of increasing economic nationalism—deliberately willed in some cases, and in others forced on reluctant Governments by the behaviour of their neighbours or by the general chaos of world economic affairs. Rising tariffs on a much higher scale than before 1914 showed the strength of this tendency; but soon there were added to tariffs all manner of devices for fostering home industries and limiting foreign competition—subsidies to manufacturers, quotas imposed upon importers, licensing systems, exchange controls which regulated foreign trade indirectly by granting or refusing the means of payment, special bilateral arrangements for the direct exchange of surplusses and for the clearing of past debts and current commercial accounts, and so on. The collapse of the gold standard and the enforced substitution of monetary 'management' for a mainly automatic regulation of financial affairs provided ready opportunities for the manipulation of foreign trade in the supposed interest of the nation; and every step taken by one Nation State led to reprisals or parallel movements by others.

All this time the swift advance of industrial technique was bringing larger and larger productive units into existence and creating an imperative need for larger markets. Many of the characteristic industries of the twentieth century— for example, the making of motor cars—cannot be carried on at all on an economic basis by a small country dependent on its home market; and some of the greatest basic industries—*e.g.* steel making—can be located only at a very high cost in countries which lack the right combinations of fuel and raw materials. This situation has tremendous military as well as economic consequences. As war became more and more a matter of intensive mechanisation—of great air fleets and panzer divisions, of oil and rubber, and of skill in the mechanical arts—the armed forces of the smaller nations grew nearly helpless against the more advanced military equipment which only a few great States could afford or command. It had been a postulate of nineteenth-century Nationalism that even small Nation States could at need put up enough resistance to the forces of their greater neighbours to make the latter think twice before attacking them, and could defend themselves long enough for allies to mobilise and come to their help. It was an unspoken postulate of the Peace Treaties of 1919 and 1920 that this condition still held good, and that alliances of small nations could possess a significant amount of military strength. But the events of 1939 and 1940 showed very plainly that these conditions had practically ceased to operate, and that a great, highly mechanised army, accompanied by a great force of fighting and bombing airplanes, could simply blast out of its way the feeble resistance which could be offered by any lesser Power, or by any possible combination of lesser Powers.

These events plainly foreshadowed the impending disappearance of a state system based on the idea of national independence as a sovereign right of men. For the Sovereign State which cannot defend itself, even for a time, against foreign attack is an obvious impostor, laying claim to an authority which it does not in fact possess. In the circumstances of to-day, the only Nation State which can in truth possess the attributes of sovereign independence is the great State; and in the case of great States surrounded by smaller neighbours it is inevitable, if State Sovereignty is to remain the basis of political relationships, that the great States should seek to engulf their neighbours, and the small States be kept alive, if at all, only when they are in the position of buffers between the great. Nationalism as a basis for the State can survive under these conditions only in its per-

D 2

verted imperialist form—that is, by expressing the will of the great nation, not to self-determination, but to imperial rule over its weaker neighbours.

Parallel to this military process of annihilation of the real political independence of the smaller nations is the economic process which makes them unable to pursue independent policies of their own in the sphere of trade and production. Dependent on their greater neighbours both for markets and for most forms of capital equipment and many kinds of essential consumers' goods, compelled to link their financial systems to one or another of the world's major currencies, and driven to render their domestic apparatus of production subservient to the needs of one or more of the major consuming countries, they can retain no real economic independence, though they can still to some extent balance between the conflicting claims of the great States. In their economic dealings with these great States, the smaller States are almost always at a disadvantage; for usually the great States have alternative sources of supply, whereas the small ones have no alternative markets. Even when a small State is in a monopoly position as a supplier of particular goods, this only renders it more an object of desire to its greater neighbours, and, while it may enable it for a time to drive harder bargains, makes its independence more precarious.

Most unhappily placed of all are the peasant countries, which cannot afford to industrialise themselves, even if they possess the requisite raw materials for developed production, but must depend for their supplies of industrial goods on the regular sale abroad of their basic agricultural products. For the world's agricultural markets are not only narrowed by protective policies designed to increase domestic output of foodstuffs and to lessen the internal differences between rural and urban standards of living, but are also for the most part so highly competitive that the peasant exporters are at a serious disadvantage, and can be compelled by a ruthless and stronger neighbour to make their exchanges on very unfavourable terms. It is notorious that the Nazis, in their dealings with these countries, have exploited their bargaining advantages with very great success. They have compelled the peasant countries to take in exchange for their food exports not what they want, but what the Nazis are ready to supply. It is time that, even so, the peasants may have profited, in the sense that if the Germans had not bought their produce it would have remained unsold. But this does not alter the fact that the great State—Germany— has been systematically exploiting the smaller States for its own economic advantage.

It would be possible to enlarge at almost any length on the absurdities of the European frontiers of 1939 from the standpoint of economic convenience and well-being. But this has been done so often that it seems unnecessary to do it yet again. It is often suggested that these absurdities are caused by the folly of the statesmen of 1919 in refusing to give sufficient weight to the economic factors. But in truth the source of the trouble goes much deeper. It was utterly beyond the bounds of possibility so to draw the frontiers of Europe that each 'nation' should constitute a separate, independent State and at the same time to preserve the essential units of economic cooperation. No doubt, this would not have mattered if the Nation States had been prepared to treat their independence as purely 'political', and to refrain from putting any barriers in the way of free intercourse—including not only the exchange of goods, but in addition free movement of capital, freedom of migration, and international coordination of transport and finance. But it was plainly out of the question that this could happen. Statehood was taken by the rulers of each State as including the right to pursue an independent economic policy ; and, though it was in practice impossible for the small States to be economically independent of the great, this limitation on their powers made them only the more determined to practise economic independence at one another's expense.

Even if the League of Nations had completely fulfilled the promise of its constitution, this would not have fundamentally altered the position. For the League was, in its very conception, a League of independent Nation States, within which certain privileges were conferred of necessity on the Great Powers, but in economic matters each State, large or small, retained the fullest nominal independence. It was doubtless intended, by using the power of the great national banks to promote a general return to the gold standard, to pin down all the League States to the observance of certain traditional rules of economic behaviour—especially to deflation at the call of the great banks ("When Father says Deflate, we all deflate"). But this in practice made matters worse; for when observance of the 'gold standard rules' imposed intolerable strains on the dislocated economies of one country after another, the inevitable outcome was a resort to extreme nationalist financial policies as the only way of checking the dissolution of the national economy and preventing the outbreak of revolutions of despair.

Pre-war Europe was, in effect, an economic monstrosity, fully as absurd, from the economic point of view, as if each State within the United States of America were to pursue a policy of complete economic independence, with tariff walls against the other States, quotas on imports, control over 'foreign' payments to other States, and a separate currency system of its own. So much was this the case that, from the purely economic point of view, it is quite arguable that it would be better to let Hitler conquer all Europe short of the Soviet Union, and thereafter exploit it ruthlessly in the Nazi interest, than to go back to the pre-war order of independent Nation States with frontiers drawn so as to cut right across the natural units of production and exchange. This is part of the reason why there is in the Nation States which Hitler has overrun no general repudiation of the Nazis' 'new economic order'. If the defeat of Germany were to mean a return to pre-war conditions, why should the peasants of Rumania or Yugoslavia desire it? May not any sort of European economic unification be, from their point of view as poor producers, better than none?

The conclusion is that it will be a sheer disaster if the victors at the end of the present war try to restore anything at all resembling the pre-war system of separate and independent Nation States. But it will be no less a disaster if the economic unification which is imperatively needed in Europe is brought about at the cost of flouting the spirit of nationality. For it is not true, even in the long run, that the economic forces are bound to prevail over the national spirit to the extent of making men content to live in a far-flung supra-national State which denies their several national aspirations. The economic forces may be strong enough to compel them to live in such a State, and they may be materially better off for doing so. But that does not mean that they will live in it happily, or contentedly, or at peace.

Our problem, then, is to find means of reconciling the national feelings and aspirations of the European peoples with the overwhelming economic, and also military, need for supra-national unity. It is the main purpose of this book to enquire into the means of doing this, and therewith to suggest the policy at which Socialists internationally, and progressives in every country, ought to aim in laying their plans for post-war reconstruction in Europe.

CHAPTER IX

THE CONDITIONS OF EUROPEAN PROGRESS

EACH INDEPENDENT or self-governing State has, within its own frontiers, to make certain dispositions of powers and functions between its central government and such local, regional and provincial governments as it recognises as repositories of a part of the public authority. When the

State is strictly 'unitary', the problem is merely one of the distribution of powers and functions between the central government and the local. When the State is fully 'federal', under a written Constitution alterable only by a special procedure designed to safeguard the 'state rights' of its constituent elements, only certain powers and functions are vested in the central authority, and all other powers belong to the smaller bodies within it. Between these extremes there are many mixed types; and special complications arise in the case of imperial States which have varying relations with more or less self-governing dominions or dependencies. There are endless possible variations in the distribution of powers; and sometimes it is impossible accurately to assign a particular constitutional set-up to any single category.

These endless varieties of governmental forms are based on all sorts of considerations and causes—economic, historical, sentimental, psychological, and even merely accidental. But the need for *some* distribution of powers, as distinct from the need for distributing them in any particular way, rests at bottom upon two factors—the administrative impracticability of complete centralisation, and the desire of men to be governed, at any rate in some matters, in small groups and by persons whose outlook has a great deal in common with their own. These considerations hold good even when there is no conscious will to democracy; but they are immensely stronger wherever such a conscious will exists. For democracy means, among other essential things, the right of the people to choose the rulers; and this power of choice has very little meaning unless it can be exercised over an area small enough for the electors to have some knowledge of those among whom they have to choose, and of the issues which their chosen delegates or representatives will have to settle. I do not mean that democracy cannot be exercised over areas too wide for these conditions to be more than rudimentarily satisfied; but I do mean that it cannot be successfully exercised over large areas unless it is being exercised over small areas as well, or unless there is a fairly close connection between these two spheres of its operation.

This is the fundamental case for local self-government, which may exist to a considerable extent inside States un-democratically governed at the centre, but is a *sine qua non* of democratic central government. Similarly, if there are to be areas of government much more extensive and diversified than those of existing Nation States, the only condition on which these larger areas can be governed democratically is that there shall be within them smaller units of democratic government, and that authority shall be distributed between the greater and the smaller administrations.

In relation to the supra-national democracy of the great State, national administration has to occupy a position analogous to that of local or regional administration inside the Nation State. But to assert this is to leave a great many alternative possibilities open. What powers and functions are to be assigned to the national, and what to the supra-national, authority? Is the supra-national authority to be really a 'State', in the sense in which the word is commonly understood now—that is, a repository of ultimate authority, or 'sovereignty', as the constitutional jurists call it? Or is it to be merely a 'certain-purposes' body, with a mandate to control certain services over its entire area, but no power outside the range of functions definitely ceded to it by its constituent 'States'?

In two fields of action at least—the military and the economic, which are 'key' functions in the societies of to-day—it seems that there must be a cession of final authority to the supra-national body. We have seen that, if armed force remains an attribute of the national grouping, this must mean in practice the entire helplessness of small nations in face of great, and is pretty certain to lead to the actual domination, or even conquest, of the former by the latter. Similarly, in the sphere of economic action, as long as each national group is theoretically free to pursue its own policy irrespective of its neighbours' interests, there will be in practice a struggle among the great nations for economic predominance, leading to the inclusion of the smaller within the economic systems of their greater neighbours. This situation will make impossible both that 'natural' division of labour between the nations which was the ideal of Adam Smith and the practical aspiration of Cobden, and the alternative of concerted planning for welfare, over areas wide enough to take full advantage of the opportunities of modern productive technique.

There is, however, a clear difference between the internationalisation of military force and the internationalisation of economic policy. In the case of armed force, it is a question of all or nothing. It will by no means serve to have *some* supra-national armed forces, existing side by side with similar forces belonging to each distinct nation. The supra-national army, navy and air force will not avail to keep the peace unless they possess overwhelming power; but if they do possess this power, of what use can separate armies, navies or air forces be to the constituent national groups? Police, indeed, may remain as a national service, merely for the prevention of internal law-breaking. But armed force capable of waging war must clearly become an exclusive possession of the supra-national authority, or it will not be able to make peace secure.

In the economic sphere, on the other hand, there is room for division of powers. It is by no means necessary to vest *all* economic authority in the hands of the supra-national government, which needs only power enough to prescribe to the constituent nations a common economic plan, and to ensure its general execution. The economic need, apart from a few very special cases, is rather for supra-national co-ordination than for direct administration by a single authority. The coordinating power must be large enough both to prevent the constituent nations from following practices which are contrary to the common interest in a general concerted plan, and also positively to lay down the broad lines of economic development for the supra-national area as a whole. But within the general principles thus defined, there is room for a retention of very extensive powers of both planning and execution in the hands of the smaller units of government.

Take, as an example of what is meant, the practical working of the system of economic planning in the Soviet Union. There is one general plan for the entire U.S.S.R.; but this plan is made up by bringing together and dovetailing a large number of smaller plans made not only by the appropriate bodies within each distinct Soviet Republic, but also by lesser bodies within the several Republics. The function of the supreme planning authority is to analyse, compare and reconcile all these partial plans, making out of them a concerted plan for the Soviet Union as a whole. The partial plans are not, of course, made without central guidance: there is at the outset a collective decision that special prominence is to be given in the forthcoming general plan, say, to improving transport facilities, or to raising the productivity of agriculture, or to the expansion of the heavy industries, or to an increased supply of manufactured consumers' goods. The successive Five Year Plans of the Soviet Union have varied in the emphasis laid on the development of this or that part of the Soviet economy; and general directions on this point have been issued at the outset, before the various appropriate bodies have set to work to formulate their sectional plans. But within this very general indication of the broad policy to be followed, the various bodies make up their plans and forward them to the central planning organisation, which thereupon proceeds to harmonise them into a single plan.

This, however, is by no means the end of the planning process. The plan, when it has been made, goes back for actual execution to the various bodies, local and functional, which have been responsible for drafting its various sections;

and every part of it remains open to continuous criticism and amendment in the light of changing conditions, or of failures at this or that point. There is continual coming and going between the central and local or sectional planners, and continual adjustment of the plan itself. Moreover, there has been a steady tendency, as the Soviet leaders have gained assurance and experience, to diminish the degree of centralisation in the practical execution of the plan, and to hand over to the various local and functional groups not only greater powers in execution, but also more freedom in the devising and adaptation of their several parts of the plan.

It is not suggested that the making, or the execution, of a common plan for the countries of Western Europe can proceed along lines at all closely similar to those of Soviet planning. The Soviet planners began both with a centralised political State, which they proceeded to make less centralised as they became better assured of its stability, and with an economic machine controlled directly by that centralised State because there was no other organ capable, in the initial stages, of controlling it and giving it the right general direction. Unless the war leads in Western Europe to an entire breakdown of the existing Nation States (I am not denying that it may do this, if it goes on long enough), the situation of post-war planners in the West will be essentially different. Their task will be rather one of coordinating economic agencies which exist already in the different national groups than of first creating a highly centralised economic machine and thereafter trying to break it up into more manageable units. In the Soviet Union, the greatest difficulty was to avoid concentrating too much power at the centre; in Western Europe it is probable that it will be rather to concentrate enough. Again, in the Soviet Union the first task of the planners was to bring about the rapid industrialisation of a vast backward area; whereas in Western Europe the basis of industrialism has been laid already, and the main tasks are to bring about a better coordination of its existing resources and to develop backward areas which are relatively few and manageable, provided that they are tackled with the united resources of the more advanced areas.

These differences are very great, and point to wide differences in methods and forms of control. But they do not override the fundamental resemblances. For in both cases it is essential to plan over a wide area for a balanced output of many different kinds of goods and services, to direct capital investment where it is most needed in order to raise the economic level of backward but promising districts, to provide a convenient system of transport and communication for men and goods over the entire territory covered by the plan, to promote in all areas a condition of 'full' and appropriate employment of the available man-power and already accumulated capital, and to secure that the resulting product shall be distributed, as far as possible, to the best social advantage. Planning in Western Europe will probably need to be a good deal less centralised than planning is, even now, in the Soviet Union. But it will need to be centralised enough to ensure the general predominance of common economic objectives.

What power must the planning authority of a supra-national State have in order to achieve this? Let us consider first the two questions round which there has been most discussion in recent years by international conferences, by the economic and financial sections of the League of Nations, and by economists laying plans for the world's future or endeavouring to apportion the blame for its mischances. These two questions are the control of foreign trade and of the mechanisms of currency and credit. Within a supra-national economic system, are the national units to be free (a) to impose tariffs or quotas, to subsidise exports, or to regulate and direct foreign trade by prohibitions, licences, discriminating arrangements, control of the means of payment, or any other devices for interfering with the 'free, flow of goods from one part of the entire area to another; (b) to retain their own currencies, with power, by 'management', to manipulate their exchange values in terms of other currencies, as a means of stimulating either exports or employment; (c) to discriminate between their own 'nationals' and the citizens of other national groups within the area or outside it, by granting or refusing rights of trade or investment or the like; or (d) if they so choose, to 'nationalise' their entire systems of foreign trading, or of banking and finance, so as to make the national group itself, or a functional authority within it, the responsible body for the conduct of this section of their economic affairs?

Clearly, if each country within the supra-national State were to retain an unlimited power to impose tariffs or to influence the course of trade by means of quotas, licences, prohibitions, subsidies, or control of payments across the national frontiers, there would be no possibility of a common supra-national plan. But it does not follow that all tariffs within the supra-national area could be immediately swept away. Tariffs serve the purpose of providing public revenue as well as protection for domestic producers; and the sudden loss of all receipts from this source would cause serious difficulties in the more backward countries, which cannot easily raise the sums they need for public purposes by direct taxation. Moreover, a sudden removal of all existing tariffs would, if production and exchange continued to be conducted on a competitive basis, involve the bankruptcy of many local industries which owe their existence to this form of protection. It is accordingly improbable that all internal tariffs could be immediately removed, unless it were regarded as best to replace them by quotas or other forms of protection, and to make up, where need arose, the loss of revenue by grants from the revenues of the supra-national body. Probably it would be thought best to leave tariffs in being for a limited period, but to require that every duty proposed for retention or imposition by a national body should need the sanction of the supra-national planning authority. A similar sanction would be needed for any proposal to impose quotas or prohibitions or licensing restrictions or controls over imports by restrictions on the means of payment. This sanctioning power could then be used for the gradual extinction of all internal obstacles to the complete unification of trading opportunities over the entire supra-national area.

The question of currencies and bank control is no less crucial. The solid advantage possessed by the gold standard was that it did in effect provide all countries which fully accepted it with a common currency. But there were also serious disadvantages; for acceptance of this international standard deprived each separate country—unless it had great resources in reserve—of the power to 'manage' its own monetary affairs in such a way as to correct tendencies making for excessive boom or for depression within its frontiers. Conscious of this defect, economists who believed in the practicability of 'evening out the trade cycle' by monetary 'management' have usually favoured national monetary independence, and have been prepared to accept the disadvantage of fluctuating foreign exchanges in order to further the preservation of internal economic stability.

This whole problem, however, takes on quite a different aspect as soon as countries, instead of competing one with another in a planless world, set to work to plan their combined economies on a basis of complementary mutual exchanges. It is plainly inconsistent with such a plan that any one country should endeavour to manipulate trade or production to its own advantage at the expense of other members of its group; and the granting of this power would evidently upset the working of the combined plan even more than the retention of complete tariff-making power. A supra-national plan requires and connotes a common currency over the entire area covered by the plan, or at any rate a system of fixed exchange rates if the various countries prefer to retain their traditional monetary units. There can be in this case no question of half-measures to be applied during a period of transition. It is all or nothing; and the situation seems clearly to call for the transference of the functions of central banking wholly and completely to the supra-national authority.

This does not imply a return to the gold standard. It is probable that the supra-national authority, covering a group of countries, will prefer to retain independence in its monetary dealings with other groups, or with separate countries outside its area. Nor would it follow, even if the entire world adopted a uniform currency, that this currency should be based upon gold. There is no need to discuss these large issues here. It is enough to show that, within such a supra-national group as we are considering, it is indispensable to bring about a complete unification of currency systems and of fundamental monetary policy.

National discrimination is also a power which evidently cannot be conceded to the individual countries within the supra-national area. Discrimination against countries outside the group would be clearly a matter for the supra-national authority itself: discrimination within the group would be inconsistent with the conditions of supra-national planning. This would not exclude special trading arrangements between neighbour countries for mutual exchange of products; but such arrangements would need the sanction of the larger authority.

The final question, of the four raised some pages back, involves much more complicated issues than the other three. It can indeed hardly be discussed without raising the much wider issue of the whole foundation on which economic planning is to rest. Can a supra-national plan be made only for a Socialist group of countries, as it has been made for the group included in the Soviet Union? Or can it be made equally, though on different lines, for a group of capitalist countries, in which production and trade are carried on mainly by way of 'private enterprise'? Or, finally, is a common plan practicable for countries of which some are Socialist and some are capitalist in their economic structure?

Even these questions do not fully cover the complexity of the issue. If capitalism remains in being, either in some or in all the countries included in the group, what are to be the relations of capitalist enterprises, and especially of those whose operations are international, to the governments of the group as a whole and of its constituent countries? If industries are to be 'socialised', are they to be owned and managed on behalf of the governments of the constituent countries or of the supra-national government? Or are some industries to be owned and controlled in one way, and some in another? These questions are plainly crucial to any intelligible account of the economics of supra-national planning. But they are so far-reaching and difficult that no full answer to them can possibly be attempted in this small book. Even so, what parts of them I can attempt to answer are complex enough to merit a chapter to themselves.

CHAPTER X

EUROPEAN TRADE AND EMPIRE

IT IS in these days an increasingly common argument in favour of private capitalism that, by making matters of international economics the affair of private persons or corporations, and not of governments, it prevents them from becoming a source of international friction and of war. Liberals hark back regretfully to the days when, they tell us, economic and political relationships were kept apart, and States made no use of their political power to pursue the economic advantage of their traders. I am not so sure as these Liberals that this golden age ever existed; but let that pass. What I am quite certain of is that no such disjunction is possible in the world of to-day or to-morrow. Whether industries are publicly or privately owned, modern Governments, as long as their States retain independent sovereignty, will use their political power as a means of pushing their foreign trade, protecting and fostering the investments of their nationals, and generally seeking national economic advantages at the expense of others. They will do this, under public or private enterprise, as long as they form parts of a world in which there exists no common economic plan for sharing out resources and developing world trade on an orderly basis of exchanges for the mutual satisfaction of needs. They will do this, because they will have no alternative to doing it, in a world which offers no rational plan to which they can conform, and also because, if one country acts in this way, others are bound in self-protection to follow suit.

The difference between Socialism and private capitalism in this respect is not that under the one the State is a party to international economic dealings and under the other not, but that under a socialised system the State appears directly as a party to such dealings, whereas under private capitalism its part in them is indirect, and often concealed. There is no possibility, in developed countries whose economies are based on modern techniques, of the Sovereign State divesting itself of interest in such matters as foreign trade and investment. If the country is Socialist in its essential institutions, these activities will be direct matters of public policy : if it is capitalist, the great combines which are inseparable from modern productive technique under capitalism will insist that the State shall intervene where they need its help, and will be in a position to insist, because the Government will not be able to stand out against their threats of slump and disaster if such demands are refused. A successful capitalist State must, in major matters, follow the policy desired by the great capitalist groups : as soon as these groups change over from desiring *laissez-faire* to desiring intervention and State-protection, the capitalist State is bound to become involved, as their champion, in international economic relations. Witness the British Trade Agreements with Scandinavian and other countries, or the British Government's action in imposing prohibitive duties on foreign steel in order to force the continental steel cartel to agree to terms acceptable to the British steelmakers.

It is not true that socialisation is bound to lead to economic frictions between States which would not exist under private enterprise. What is true is that, as the scramble for markets grows more intense and capitalist concentration reaches larger dimensions, questions which would have remained largely outside politics at an earlier period become intensely political, and lead to inter-State disputes between rival capitalist groups, each using its own State as an instrument of economic power.

In a capitalist world, there is no way of resolving these quarrels except by fighting them out (or of course compromising where the issues at stake are not too difficult). There is no possibility of removing the source of disputes by setting out to organise the world, or a large section of it, on a planned basis of agreed international exchanges, or of transcending the limits of States except by means of irresponsible international capitalist compacts designed to exploit the consumers. There is indeed a serious danger that a supra-national State, composed of countries still working under systems of private enterprise, would in practice be dominated in matters of economic policy by the great internationally organised cartels and trusts, to the detriment both of the consuming public and of the lesser industries organised upon a narrower, national basis.

We can, then, dismiss the contention that Socialism is dangerous because it would lead to economic friction between States. The plain truth is that this friction exists now, between rival capitalisms, and is transcended only when international rings of capitalists organise themselves for exploiting the peoples on a supra-national scale. Socialism, so far from being a cause of international economic friction, is the only available instrument for doing away with it by replacing the machinations of groups of profit-makers by planned development of economic relations in the interests of the whole body of consumers in the countries affected.

All this, however, is merely a preliminary clearing of the ground for the main discussion proposed for this chapter. Let me re-state that question. Can a supra-national plan be made only for a group of Socialist countries, or can it be made equally well for a group of capitalist countries, or for a group including both Socialist and capitalist countries? In practice, I am sure, the close economic relations proposed in the last chapter are possibly only between countries which have a common basis of economic organisation. I should qualify this by agreeing that, given the common basis for the main countries included in the group, it would be quite possible for countries having a somewhat different basis to attach themselves to it loosely—as, for example, Outer Mongolia is attached to the Soviet Union. But I should deny entirely that any real supra-national planning is possible except among countries which have in the main a common set of economic institutions.

These institutions, I should say further, must be fundamentally Socialist, to the extent of resting on the social ownership of the key industries and services—at least of banking, of long-distance transport, of the land, of the main sources of power supply, and probably of the heavy and main constructional industries as well. Nor is it enough for supra-national planning that these key services should be publicly owned by the Government of the constituent countries. What is needed, at least for banking and main-line transport, and power supply, and probably for certain sections of the constructional industries—those making aircraft, ships, railway material, and the basic materials used in these industries—is supra-national ownership and direct control under the auspices of the supra-national authority, which would thus, incidentally, control also the main sources of armament-making. For in this particular group of services, and also probably in the supply of oil and some other essential materials, the need would be not merely to coordinate national plans of development, but to carry out and administer actual supply systems extending over the whole supra-national area. The railway system, the air services, the shipping, the postal communications, the electric power supply of Western Europe ought all to be planned on a more than national basis, and administered by common authorities covering the widest possible area. This would not, of course, exclude the power to delegate the working of any part of these services to national or smaller authorities—for example, the distribution of electric current to consumers as distinct from the planning and management of a supra-national electric 'grid', or the running of a particular railway line serving purely localised needs. But the supra-national authority, and not the smaller bodies within its area, must over all this range of services have the deciding voice about what is to be delegated, and what is to be centrally controlled.

Another field of action in which the final power must clearly pass to the supra-national authority is that of colonial economic development. Decisions about industrialisation in colonial territories, as part of a general economic plan, must clearly rest in the hands of the central planning authority. I am not directly discussing in this chapter the future political government of the colonial empires of the countries entering into the supra-national union. That is another question; but, whatever their political future, it is clear that, if colonies continue to be attached to the countries belonging to the supra-national union, either severally or to the union itself, the separate countries cannot be left with power to promote their economic development except in accordance with the requirements of the supra-national plan. To the extent to which colonial territories become self-governing dominions within the union, the situation is slightly different; for such dominions would clearly rank as full members of the union, though a special status might have to be accorded to them, and special arrangements made, where their geographical position and existing economic relations linked them up closely, in an economic sense, with countries or groups outside the area of the union (*e.g.* Canada, in relation to the United States; India, in relation to the Far East, or, possibly, to the Soviet Union).

This unification of colonial territories is of vital importance. To say nothing of Great Britain, such countries as Holland, Belgium and Portugal, which possess large and distant colonial empires populated by subject native peoples, would present an insoluble problem if they were to retain these possessions for themselves within a supranational union. They clearly cannot hope, if the question is to be one of brute force, to retain their empires by their own strength; and they are clearly not entitled to use the united strength of West European democracy in order to retain them for themselves alone. The development of these colonies, as far as they remain attached to Europe at all, is plainly a matter to be handled in terms of a common plan for the development of mutual trade between them and the industrialised areas of Europe, for planned export of their surpluses to other parts of the world, and for planned investment designed to develop their resources and to improve their standards of life.

Nor is this less true of the colonies belonging to the major empires of France and Great Britain. But in these areas the position is rather complex. A large part of the French Empire consists of territories in Northern Africa which have been partly 'assimilated' to France itself, and in one case, Algeria, governed as a province of the metropolitan country. There is clearly no reason why, if French people are prepared to accord to the citizens of such territories complete equality of political rights, and if the citizens themselves consent, they should not be treated as parts of France, and enter on this footing into the supra-national union of Western Europe. This, however, would have to be strictly conditional on the concession of equal rights; for it would be impracticable to have 'subjects', as distinct from 'citizens', living in any part of the area represented by the supra-national authority. As for the remaining French colonies—those distant from France and those unwilling to accept complete assimilation—they would, with the colonies of the other European countries concerned, either gain their independence or become units in the colonial territory attached to the supra-national union itself.

In the case of the British Empire, the chief complications are those arising in India and South Africa. The other Dominions could, as they wished, either proclaim their economic independence, or become units in the new supra-national authority, or attach themselves to some other supra-national group. But South Africa, because of the race cleavage which exists within its borders, would be ineligible for membership of the supra-national authority, and would be called upon to purge itself of race-discrimination as a condition of membership. The result would probably be a break-away which would leave the Union of South Africa to make the best of its independence in face of a rising tide of African cultural development fostered by the supra-national union as an essential part of its policy of colonial emancipation.

India, on the other hand, would have a choice between an independence unmarred by racial inequality and entry into the economic system which has its centre in the Soviet Union. It could hardly enter as a unit into the supra-national union of Western Europe, from which it is too widely sundered not merely by distance but, much more, by differences of social tradition and structure and of standards and habits of life. As an independent country, or rather group of countries—for it is in itself a supra-national area—it could enter into treaty relationships with both

Western Europe and the Soviet Union, on terms which would ensure its rapid economic development with the aid of European capital and technical resources. Or alternatively it might simply join forces with the Soviet Union, almost certainly carrying with it some of the smaller independent countries of the Near and Middle East, and possibly even China and Japan. It is, however, probable that in the long run India is destined to be the centre of a great supra-national State covering the whole of the Middle East, and lying between a Sino–Japanese Far Eastern Soviet Republic, a Near Eastern State based on Egypt, Turkey, and Arabia, and the Soviet Union to the North. What is barely imaginable is that in any circumstances India should either remain attached specifically to Great Britain, or become, like the self-governing British Dominions, a unit in a supra-national State with its centre in Western Europe.

I am well aware that colonial exploitation is no more defensible when it is carried out by a supra-national State than when it is practised by Nation States individually. It would be of no advantage to the colonial peoples to be merely transferred from British or French or Dutch or Portuguese rule to the rule of a West European union, if the new authority were merely to carry on the policy of its predecessors. Indeed, this might be a serious disadvantage, by putting additional obstacles in the way of native revolt. The continuance of 'colonies' in any form is defensible only because there are areas in which there exists at present no means of creating native Governments of a kind or on a scale corresponding to the minimum requirements of twentieth-century statehood. Negro Africa is plainly destined, at some time in the future, to become the home of a supra-national State possessing full independence. But it would be mere Utopianism to pretend that such a State could be brought into being at once, either by deliberate creation from outside, or as an outcome of native rebellion against foreign rule. There does not exist in negro Africa the political consciousness that is needed to provide the foundations for such a State; and the creation of it is bound therefore to be a matter of time. Meanwhile, a way must be found of governing negro Africa so as to lead as quickly as possible to complete self-government.

Can anyone in his senses suppose that such a policy would ever be pursued by a supra-national authority working within the conditions of capitalist production? For the capitalist, native labour and native resources of raw materials and potential wealth are simply means to the making of profits; and considerations of native welfare arise only to the extent to which they must be borne in mind by the prudent profit-seeker, or at all events only to the extent to which they are consistent with extracting the maximum profit. States, including supra-national States, could of course impose legal restrictions on the capitalist exploiter, by passing laws regulating wages, hours of labour, and so on. But they could not, if they relied on capitalist concerns to develop native production, proceed with such legislation to a point at which the capitalists would seriously object to it; for if they did enterprises would be abandoned, and working capital withdrawn, with the consequence of leaving the native population much worse off than if no development had ever taken place. If the capitalist is to take the risks of developing production in backward areas, the right to exploit native labour and resources as suits him best cannot, save within very narrow limits, be denied him. For this reason the idea of an international system of mandates, under which a supra-national authority is to govern native peoples for their own benefit, and develop native resources with a view to native welfare, is self-contradictory, where the supra-national authority is itself capitalist in economic structure and policy.

No solution of the colonial question on terms consistent with democratic principle and the spirit of international fraternity is, then, possible within the framework of capitalism. Only an international Socialist régime, keenly animated by the ideas of human rights and democratic equality of all peoples, can hope successfully to tackle the problem of colonial exploitation; because, resting in its home policy not on profit-making or on exploitation of one class by another, but on the practice of mutual service, it will naturally tend to apply its methods of fair exchange in its dealings with other peoples.

I conceive, then, of a colonial department of the European supra-national authority, administering the affairs of all colonial possessions previously attached to the separate Nation-States, wherever the link has not been severed either by the achievement of full independence by the hitherto dependent peoples (e.g. India), or by the transference of an emancipated colony to membership of some other supra-national group (e.g. Hong Kong to China, or perhaps the West Indies to a North American Union). I conceive of this colonial department as receiving a mandate to prepare the colonies under its control for self-government by the most rapid stages, and meanwhile as making plans for their economic and cultural development. I conceive of these plans, in their economic aspect, as designed to promote, not those forms of development which will best serve the interests of the European countries concerned, but rather the colonies' own advancement towards higher standards of living. I do not mean that the colonial administration could afford to ignore the economic requirements of the European markets. Clearly it could not. But it would lay its plans for the colonial economies as much in the interests of the native peoples as could be made consistent with the need to find markets for their goods—and it would seek to associate native citizens with its work of administration to the fullest possible extent.

That a supra-national Socialist State *could* set out to exploit colonies in the exclusive interests of its home population I agree. But I claim both that it is much less likely to do this than any union of capitalist States, and that it would be in a much better position for avoiding this exploitation, because its whole economy would be based on planning for maximum production and fair distribution of the products of its peoples. There is no *guarantee* of fair dealing ; but where no conceivable system can afford a guarantee, it is reasonable to prefer that which offers the least temptation to sin against the spirit of human brotherhood.

CHAPTER XI

THE SHAPE OF THE NEW EUROPE

I HAVE argued in the preceding chapter that a common basis of economic and social institutions is essential for any group of countries which is proposing to establish a supranational government, or to undertake a concerted plan of economic development over a supra-national area. Unless some countries are to be subordinated to others by sheer conquest, or by compulsion under the threat of conquest, and are thus to be forced to accept plans imposed upon them by the conquerors, the concerted development of a more than national society involves the existence of supranational governing and planning institutions which must rest on the same broad principles in all the constituent countries. Without this no real common plan is feasible, and it is out of the question either to prevent economic antagonisms or to make the best of the economic resources which are available for the use of the citizens. A plan agreed upon by countries having quite different internal economic and social structures might, indeed, be better than no plan at all. But it would be disastrously weakened by the impossibility of really coordinated development over the whole supra-national area.

This consideration, however, does not at all exclude the possibility of close commercial relations between groups of

E

countries having widely different economic and social structures. Such groups can most fruitfully enter into mutual agreements for the exchange of their surplus products, and for the dovetailing of their several economic plans. There is no valid reason why a Socialist Europe should not have quite close economic relations with a non-Socialist United States, or the European groups enter into carefully devised trade treaties with countries outside for the development of trading relations. This is a very different matter from devising and putting into execution a really concerted economic plan. It is of the greatest importance that there should be trade relations of this sort between the supra-national States of the future. But it is an error to confound such relations with combined planning, which demands the unification of certain 'key' services under a common supra-national control.

For effectiveness, the area covered by a concerted plan needs to be wide, but not without limits which can be broadly defined. The Soviet Union is, by itself, an area quite large enough for the formulation and execution of a satisfactory plan. Indeed, a wider area would have raised for the Soviet planners very serious problems of manage-ability, and might have wrecked the plan by posing too complicated questions to those responsible for it. Similarly the United States is by itself a territory large enough for effective planning. Plans have to be kept within the limits set by human capabilities, or they will break down in practice, however excellent they may look on paper. Neither the Soviet Union nor the United States could, without great economic loss, make a plan on a basis of entire economic self-sufficiency. But that is neither necessary nor desirable. Planning should not be planning for isolation, but rather a means of promoting useful exchanges between the areas covered by complementary plans.

As between such areas, a much smaller degree of similarity of economic and social institutions is necessary than between countries which are to form units within the area covered by a single plan. Exchanges can be arranged, on fair terms, between Socialist and non-Socialist areas, provided only that both have organised compatible methods of carrying on international trade. A Socialist group can even carry on quite close economic relations with a group which has no collective organisation for trading purposes. The Soviet Union has not been precluded from trading with capitalist countries merely because it trades through publicly organised commercial institutions, whereas they do not. Certain difficulties no doubt arise in the course of such relations ; but they are not insuperable. They have in fact in many instances been overcome without much friction.

It is, however, beyond doubt true that countries, or groups of countries, which have similar economic institutions, can trade with one another more easily than those which have not. A State trading monopoly can deal more easily with a parallel buying or selling organisation than with a number of separate buyers or sellers ; and, as between monopolies, satisfactory relations will be easier when both sides accept the same general principles. But these similarities are advantages only, and not positive necessities. It is not imperative to convince the American people of the necessity of Socialism before establishing reasonably satisfactory trading relations between them and a Socialist Europe.

Nor is it necessary, or perhaps even desirable at the present stage, that all Europe should be covered by a single, unified economic plan. If the Soviet Union is large enough, and diversified enough, to form a satisfactory planning unit—at any rate for some time to come—there is room in the rest of Europe for more than one plan, and for more than one group of countries committed to concerted economic and social planning on a common institutional basis. It is quite possible to conceive of a situation in which there would be one plan for Central, Eastern and South-Eastern Europe, west of the U.S.S.R., and another plan for

Western Europe—that is, three plans for Europe as a whole, including certain attached territories outside the European continent. In order to get the full benefit of concerted planning under these conditions, it would be necessary for these groups to enter into close relations both one with another and with the United States—or perhaps with a wider group including Latin America as well. But these mutual arrangements could be made without the need for each of the related plans to rest upon a common institutional foundation, or to be sponsored by political parties having closely similar constitutions and methods of government.

Indeed, planning in post-war Europe can hardly be made workable except on some such basis as this. To plan for all Europe, even apart from the Soviet Union, would be too formidable a task, unless the Soviet Union had spread its own planning area over a larger part of the continent than at present seems likely. It would be task enough, in Western Europe, to devise and administer a common plan covering, say, Great Britain, Scandinavia, Holland, Belgium, France, Spain, Portugal, Switzerland, Italy, and perhaps one or two other countries. Germany, Austria, Hungary, Czechoslovakia, Poland and the Balkan countries would form a second planning group quite as large as could be effectively unified, either politically or economically, at the present stage of human development in the arts of government and administration. To attempt more than this would be to court disaster on account of the dangers of bureaucracy and over-centralisation.

Be it understood that I am not putting forward these actual groupings as more than hypothetical examples. I do not pretend to know either how far westward the economic and political influence of the Soviet Union will extend after the war, or how precisely the countries of Western, Central, Southern and Eastern Europe will group themselves, either politically or in their economic relations. All I am suggesting is that there does seem to be a possibility of these groupings, with the Soviet Union, Germany, and the Western Parliamentary countries as their respective rallying points, and that this triple division offers positive advantages, in that each of these groups could rest on a sufficient compatibility of fundamental institutions to make concerted planning effective, whereas a wider grouping probably could not, at any rate for a long time to come.

I am conscious, at this point, of begging a very large question—that of the British Empire. Will Great Britain be prepared to enter into a planning unit based on Western Europe; and, if so, will the British Dominions come in, too? With the question of India and the Colonies I have dealt in the preceding chapter; but the position of Australia, New Zealand, Canada and South Africa raises a different set of issues. There is, moreover, the wide question of the future economic and political relations of Great Britain with the United States. It is quite on the cards that Great Britain, with the British Dominions, instead of entering into a supra-national State system based on Western Europe, will become an economical and political satellite of the United States, and that Europe will have to make its plans without the participation of the British Empire.

I recognise this possibility; but I do not propose to discuss it. The new organisation of Western Europe will, of course, be very different, if Great Britain plays no part in it. In that event, the economic and political leadership in it is bound to fall to France; and the entire political future of France is so uncertain that little can usefully be said about it at the present stage. For my own part, despite the demonstrated rottenness of French politics and the manifest tiredness of the French people—more exhausted as it was than any other by the strain of the last war—I have so much faith in French civilisation as to believe that the French, when they have had their revolution and purged themselves of their petty corruptions and learnt to take their politics seriously, as they used to do, will resume their place in the advance guard of Western progress. They cannot do this without a revolutionary change, or except under entirely new leadership; for the collapse of 1940 was unmistakably the collapse of an entire régime. But the German occupation and the attack on the Soviet Union seem likely between them to end the disastrous cleavage within the French Left; and I have confidence enough in the spirit of the French people to believe that what will arise out of the ashes of the Third Republic and the puppet régime of Petain and Laval will be a force essentially democratic and civilising, and capable of playing a creative rôle in the making of the new Europe.

If Great Britain comes into the new West-European system, Great Britain and France will share the leadership of it; and the common citizenship which the British Government proposed to Frenchmen at the eleventh hour will be realised in a wider unity of the Western peoples. If not, France will stand by itself as the great cultural leader of the Western liberal forces.

To say this is enough to make plain how important it is for the future of European democracy that Great Britain shall not stand aside. For it will be immensely harder for France alone than for France and Great Britain together to give a constructive lead to Western Europe towards a Socialism imbued with the ideas of liberal democracy. France cannot easily lead either Spain or Italy, which are Latin countries: nor can France alone easily give the right lead to the Scandinavians or the Dutch. Great Britain and France together can, if they are animated by a common idea, and working on the basis of a common set of fundamental institutions. To build up close relations between the progressive forces in France and Great Britain is a hard task under present conditions. But it is a task of immense importance for the future of Europe. For upon the decision of these relations may depend the decision whether Great Britain is or is not to stand aside from the work of European reconstruction, and is or is not to become a satellite of the United States.

I can see no clear prospect of a satisfactory settlement in Europe that leaves out Great Britain as an active partner. Of course, if Great Britain, drawn by imperial and capitalist influences, does turn to the United States rather than to Europe, the work of European reconstruction will have to go on none the less. But it will be immensely harder; and if France, unaided by Great Britain, fails to play the creative rôle that is required, the possibility of a liberal Socialist grouping in Western Europe will disappear, and the three-fold basis of European planning will vanish with it, leaving Western Europe to be dominated by Germany, irrespective of the military outcome of the war. Wars do not settle who are to be the dominant peoples, save in a secondary sense. If the Germans were to win the war, they would no doubt dominate Europe, but as a result not of their victory, but of the qualities that have caused them to win. They might dominate Europe no less if they were defeated in arms, were no other countries ready or able to assume the rôle of leadership.

It will be a disaster if Great Britain 'contracts out' of the new Europe. The possibility that this may happen depends on the survival of capitalism as the dominant force in British politics. For the main thing that will drive Great Britain towards America, and away from Europe, is the hope of using the American connection as a means of keeping the capitalist system in effective power. Continental capitalism, I have argued elsewhere in this book, is incapable of being restored to its old authority. Its very foundations have been undermined. But this is much less true of British capitalism, which remains still in possession of all the key controls of the national economic life. To shake this power of British capitalism—now, while the war is in progress—is not only necessary for the sake of the war effort, but also vitally important as a means of committing Great Britain to do its part in the work of European reconstruction. British Labour, to the extent to which it pursues a constructive policy and aims at the realities of power, will turn towards Europe and not towards American capitalism. Everything that strengthens the effective hold of Labour in British politics both reinforces European Socialism, of which Great Britain is now the sole asylum, and impels Great Britain towards identification with the European democratic cause. I wish the British Labour Party showed more awareness of its mission in this respect: it is at all events a step in the right direction that the Trades Union Congress has set up a joint council with the Trade Unions of the Soviet Union. But that is not enough. The British Labour movement ought already to be taking the lead, in close association with the Soviet Union, in preparing the forces of revolution in Europe. It will not get Socialism here, unless it works for Socialism as the basis of European as well as of purely British reconstruction.

CHAPTER XII

THE CLAIMS OF NATIONALITY

Economic factors have been considered at some length in the foregoing chapters, almost to the exclusion of other factors which are of no less importance in determining the immediate future. I want now to come back to a vital issue which, I expect, has been much in many of my readers' minds. It is easy enough to make out a clear case showing the importance, on economic grounds, of achieving supra-national unity in Europe, and the sheer necessity of achiev-ing it if backward peoples are to be lifted out of primary poverty or advanced peoples to be rescued from insecurity and unemployment due to the poverty of the markets in which they seek to sell their goods. All this is easy enough; but it does not answer the vital question 'Will men do it?' Will men be able so to overcome their nationalist exclusive-ness as positively to struggle to bring about a wider unity; or will they, on the contrary, remain so determinedly exclusive and hostile to 'foreign rule' that they will sooner submit to foreign force and be conquered by their more powerful neighbours than join hands voluntarily in a supra-national order designed both to outlaw war and to prevent economic insecurity? In other words, are men so blindly nationalistic that only a Hitler or some alternative Juggernaut can combine them over a wide enough area to conform to the needs of modern technique?

It is possible that men are 'pig-headed' to this degree—in which case I should still want to overthrow Hitler in the hope that European unification might come at the hands of a victorious Soviet Union. But I am loth to credit the existence of so much folly and so little wisdom as this conclusion implies. I do believe it possible to get the peoples, under Socialist leadership, to work for supra-national unity. But I am sure they will not do this unless the supra-national order is so designed as to make ample provision for the satisfaction of real national needs.

What are the claims of nationality, when one has disentangled from them claims which rest on the identification of its essence with the achievement of complete political independence for a national State? In the first place, any group which feels itself to be a nation wants the fullest freedom to use its own language—the language that comes natural to it and embodies an important part of its cultural tradition. It wants this language to be employed in official, as well as private, affairs. It wants its laws written and interpreted in this language: it wants this language spoken in its courts, police stations, and administrative offices. It wants the teaching of this language to be basic in its schools, and the teaching of other subjects to be carried on in this language. It wants newspapers to be published, books written, dramas performed, in this language. In other words, it wants its traditional tongue to be unmistakably the language of the country. Nationalist movements among subject peoples may go beyond this, and seek to boycott altogether what they regard as the language of their conquerors; but I am not aware that any self-governing nation objects to the teaching or use of languages other than its own, provided the primacy of its own language is admitted and practically assured.

Secondly, in close connection with these linguistic aspirations, nationalists want their schools to be places where the young are taught to understand and value the national history and traditions, and to master the national values and ideas of living. They want national Universities to continue these processes, and cultural institutions of every sort to be imbued with a sense of national aspiration and achievement. They want those arts in which there is a tradition of national excellence to be especially cultivated: and they want poets, painters, musicians, sculptors and architects alike to celebrate the peculiar virtues of the national spirit. Of course, this purely cultural side of nationalism is much stronger in some cases than in others. But it is nearly always present in some degree—usually with a certain archaeological flavour when nationalists are endeavouring to revive a submerged or weakened nationalism by appeals to the past.

Thirdly, nationalists commonly claim the right to follow the traditional religion of their nation. This is a much less definable claim than those discussed already; for it may range from a mere demand for freedom of worship and religious organisation to a claim for the exclusive practice of the national religion and its secure establishment by the State as the sole religion of the people. Some nationalists will be content with freedom of worship, provided that it carries with it the right to organise a national Church with native priests and prelates and a liturgy in the national language. Some, on the other hand, will assert that a people cannot be firmly bound together without full community of religious observance, and that no one who is not in communion with the national Church can truly share in the common traditions of the people. Moreover, some religions are by profession tolerant, and others intolerant; and this makes a great difference to nationalist claims on their behalf. Some Churches are purely national, whereas others are national sections of international Churches, such as the Catholic. Some Churches are much more Erastian in doctrine than others; and this affects the nature of their relations to nationalist politicians. Whereas in the case of language and lay culture most nationalist movements make closely similar claims, in the case of religion there are endless varieties of demand.

Now, there seems to be no good reason why the linguistic and cultural claims of nationalism should not be fully reconcilable with the needs of the supra-national State, wherever such a State is based, not on imperialism, but on the will to deal fairly with all the citizens. But in the case of religion other important considerations arise. The claim that a nation must, if it is to preserve and get the full value of its national traditions, profess collectively a uniform national religion is inconsistent with the right of individual and group self-expression which all democratic state machinery ought to safeguard and to encourage. These rights are, indeed, at variance with any claim that a particular set of religious observances ought to be established by law, or that the professors of a particular set of beliefs ought to enjoy any special privileges or preferences in the educational system or in any other part of the machinery of government and administration. Churches and Governments ought to be entirely separate: there ought to be no confounding of the persons of ecclesiastical and secular jurisdiction. The Elizabethan Act of Uniformity, as an attempt to build up a broad church to which the great majority of the people could be induced to subscribe, may have been justifiable as a necessary compromise. The thoroughgoing Erastianism of Rousseau's attempt to formulate the idea of a State Church, based on the broadest sort of Deism, may have been a natural element in the first foundation of the theory of democratic sovereignty. But neither the one nor the other is consistent with a developed conception of the requirements of a democratic society. It is fundamental to the very idea of such a society that, so far from enforcing uniformity or, on a more advanced plane, recognising a particular 'establishment' while extending 'toleration' to 'dissenters', it should value the presence in its midst of widely different interpretations of man's spiritual nature.

It is, however, no less true that there must be limits to this recognition of the value of differences. These limits are set by the moral notions which are at the root of the common civilisation which holds the nation together. A Church which advocated cannibalism as a religious rite would clearly exclude itself from recognition in any advanced or democratic society. But so, I hold, does any Church which denies, as part of its basic doctrine, the right of men to worship God in their own way, or not to worship God at all, or which claims that the State ought to prohibit to all citizens practices which it condemns on the score of its religious belief. I am not, of course, denying the right of, say, Catholics to condemn divorce or birth control, or to do their best to get their views adopted by the societies in which they live. But I am condemning any claim that the Catholic, or any other, Church ought to be given power itself to enforce such doctrines, or to act in any matter as the agent for their enforcement. A Catholic has as much right as anyone else to express any view he pleases, and to endeavour to persuade others to accept his view. But no religious body has any right to exercise any coercive power over persons who do not belong to it, or to be entrusted by the State with any coercive authority.

In practice, it may be necessary, in the existing state of opinion, to admit certain limited compromises. Where the great majority of a nation belong to a particular Church, it may be unavoidable to allow that Church some part in the public ceremonials of the people in the celebration of national festivals, for example. But it would be altogether a mistake to stretch the compromise to the point of allowing any national Church to insist on membership as a qualification for any office, for admission to any University or other public institution, or for any right of citizenship; and it would be wholly indefensible to endow any such Church with any control over public education, or any power at all over any persons not voluntarily belonging to it.

The reason for this is that freedom of opinion, and the equal right to hold all opinions not directly excluded by the basic conditions of the civilisation, rank among the absolute requirements of democracy. This freedom is accordingly a right which needs to be fully safeguarded by the charter of the supra-national authority, and one which no national group can legitimately invade. Subject to this, each national group should have the right, as part of its cultural autonomy, to develop its religious institutions in its own way, recognising such varieties of religious belief, national or international, as any of its citizens may profess, and allowing the adherents of any Church to link its worship as they please either to the culture of the nation, or to the developing wider culture that transcends national frontiers.

This freedom is essential to the sense of cultural autonomy. But there are other aspects of nationality, besides those which I have discussed so far, which must be safeguarded if the peoples are to live at ease within the framework of a supra-national society. Not least among them is the right to have their affairs administered in their own language, by public officers who speak that language as natives and have as part of their mental make-up the traditions of the nation. It would no doubt greatly simplify the unification of Europe if all Europeans spoke the same language—spoke it, I mean, as their native language and not merely as a foreign language learnt for convenience of intercourse. It would be a considerable convenience if all Europeans—or indeed all peoples throughout the world—had a common second

language in addition to their own, and could thus communi-
cate one with another without interpreters in all the simpler
affairs of life. But language is not only a means of matter-
of-fact communication, but also an invaluable instrument
of thought and a rich repository of sentiment; and the full
understanding of one another's minds is something very
different from the ability to make and answer inquiries
about the times of trains, or even to exchange specialised
technical information without error. Oratory, as well as
literature, depends on the fine appreciation of language, to
which few can attain for any tongue save that which is
native to them. Each nation's language is a storehouse of the
thoughts and emotions of many generations of men; and no
people can afford to discard its own language in its public
affairs without heavy loss of social content and tradition.

It is therefore futile to propose the deliberate adoption
of any one language, whether it be an existing national
language or one invented or adapted for the purpose (e.g.
Esperanto, or Basic English), as the official language of
public affairs throughout the territories of a supra-national
State. There is much to be said for the universal acquisition,
for purposes of factual convenience, of a second language.
But, whether this is done or not, the national languages
must remain, not only as instruments of literature, but also
as the current languages of administration in the various
national areas. Conceivably, in course of generations, a
second language, taught throughout the supra-national area,
could be used for many purposes for which it could not be
used to-day. But it could not become the universal language
of public affairs until men had learnt, over the entire area,
to think instinctively in it, or until it had itself developed, as
a result of such thinking, into a real supra-national language
expressing the thoughts and sentiments and traditions of
closely unified peoples.

Nor is the question one of language only. Local affairs
must be administered mainly by men and women who share

the cultural traditions and outlook of the men and women whose lives are affected by their doings. A national group will not have the sense of collective freedom if a large proportion of those who hold public offices in its midst are foreigners—even though these foreigners may speak their second language exceedingly well. They want to be governed by persons of their own sort in all matters which closely and directly affect their individual lives and involve personal contacts between the administrator and the citizen.

These are, I believe, the essential non-economic conditions of national contentment under supra-national co-ordination. They involve, especially, national control of schools, courts of law, institutions of social service, cultural institutions, and of the entire apparatus of local and regional government. Moreover, in the economic field, though certain key services must be actually administered over the whole of the supra-national area, it is of vital importance to avoid in the great majority of services any centralisation of actual management. Coordination of plans does not involve centralised administration; and spontaneity and democratic initiative cannot be secured where centralisation is allowed to proceed beyond what is imperatively required by considerations of technique. The small unit is valuable in itself, as a liberating influence upon the human spirit; and the vaster the scale of production and distribution that is enforced on men by the advances of applied science, the more important it becomes to miss no opportunity of breaking up administration into manageable units, in which the individual can hope to exert a significant influence.

I believe that in the foregoing pages I have set down the real requirements of nationality as a basic psychological force. But the case as I have stated it is of course very far from meeting the claims of nationalist politicians, or of political nationalism as a whole. The nationalist politicians want national politics to be important in the eyes of the people: they want an abundance of high offices for themselves and their friends, and they want power. They have convinced themselves, with much truth as long as a capitalist social order is taken for granted, that the true national values can be maintained only if they are protected by a fully independent Nation State, with its own entire sovereignty in law-making as well as internal administration, its own show of force (even if the reality is impossible), and its entire freedom from any supra-national interference with its political system, its internal economic affairs, and its structure of class-relationships. They aim at persuading their nationalist followers that the spirit of nationality can be conserved and expressed only by the achievement and maintenance of complete national sovereignty.

But is this what their followers really want? The politicians have a natural impulse to want it, because it increases their sense of importance and their real power if they are small men. A big man may find satisfaction in working cooperatively within the greater, supra-national unity: a small man will want to be boss over an area small enough for him to manage. Better to reign in 'Serbonia' than serve in Europe! For the peoples, on the other hand, there is no similar prospect of self-aggrandisement in the small national unit. Even the local 'boss' is not less, but rather more, a boss if his local organisation forms part of a supra-national organisation than if it is related merely to a national unit. And, if this is true of local leaders, it is true much more of the great mass of the people.

Why, then, are nationalist leaders able to bamboozle so many followers into a belief that the successful expression of the national spirit requires an independent national Sovereign State? They can do this, because up to the present it has been so largely true. Ireland could never have achieved full cultural freedom (which is none the less freedom for having been abused in a number of ways) without achieving first, not merely Home Rule, but in effect independent sovereignty. The same is true of Poland, of Czechoslovakia, of Finland—indeed, of all the Nation States in Europe which have succeeded in freeing themselves from political subjection to their larger neighbours. Historically, it is true that, in Western Civilisation generally, national rights of self-development and expression could be won only by winning first complete emancipation from foreign rule.

This has set up very powerful psychological forces which drive nationalists to an assertion of the necessity of full political independence. But it does not follow that the one does of necessity involve the other. Independence of a domineering conqueror intent on imposing his national culture upon his subject peoples is one thing—independence of a supra-national authority based on the idea of equal cooperation between many national cultures is quite another. If the supra-national authority is itself neither nationalist nor nationalist-imperialist, but international in spirit and structure, there is no valid reason why the nationalities included within its scope should not find the fullest opportunity for national self-expression without either sovereign independence or exclusive national control in the economic field.

It will, however, not be easy to persuade men of this, in face of the attitude of nationalist leaders. There will be in many quarters an instinctive identification of the cause of national freedom with the restoration of national Governments which have been driven into exile by the Nazis. It may turn out to be a great blessing when, as in the case of France, no such exiled Government exists, and there is accordingly no vested claim of monarch or sovereign institution to be put back into power. Elsewhere, there is very grave danger that victory over Hitler may mean a British–American attempt to reinstate in authority Kings and Governments which are quite unsuitable for the tasks of building up the new Europe.

These dangers may, no doubt, be averted by the plain

refusal of the peoples of Holland and Belgium, Norway and
Poland, Yugoslavia and Greece, and the rest of them to have
back their exiled authorities at any price. I hope it will. But
I also hope that exiled Socialists will avoid any action that
could make them parties to attempts at restoring the pre-
war Nation States with their old institutions and their discredited monarchs and Governments. It is the duty of
Socialists to think internationally about the problems of
European reconstruction, and not to allow the necessities
of war cooperation to twist their thinking out of its proper
course.

I admit that the difficulties are considerable. It is necessary for the Socialist exiles not only to collaborate with anti-
Socialists of their own nations in the task of winning the war,
but also to do what they can to stir up revolutions in their
own countries on a basis which will arouse nationalist as
well as Socialist sentiment. If Revolutions come in Western
Europe either during or at the end of the war, they are
bound to have to a large extent a nationalist character;
for success in revolution involves mobilising all the powerful
forces of discontent. The Socialists may therefore be compelled to struggle for national restoration in the first instance, rather than for Socialism directly. What they have
to do is, while playing their part in this national struggle, to
stress continually the need for more than national collaboration in creating the new Europe, and to insist that, in the
course of the national struggle, the future form of the State
shall be left an open question, to be determined by the
expressed will of the people when the national freedom of
decision has been won back in arms.

This, to be sure, involves the danger that the people,
when the time comes, will elect for national sovereignty
rather than for national freedom within a supra-national
order. But whether this will be so or not will depend, partly
on the force of events, but also partly on the success with
which the Socialists of neighbouring countries practise

collaboration and plan for it as the basis of their respective societies. If they fail to practise and to plan for supranational collaboration now, the victory will for the immediate post-war period be likely to go by default to the political Nationalists, and Socialism itself will be submerged. For the victory of this type of Nationalism will mean also the victory of capitalism, of which it is one of the political expressions.

Even, however, if, by the failure of the Socialists, a narrow Nationalism is allowed the immediate victory, this will not end the matter. For the nominally wholly 'independent' Nation States will not, in practice, be able to maintain their independence. In the immediate post-war period they will have to be fed, clothed, rehabilitated by some sort of supranational authority; for these tasks will be entirely beyond their separate, independent power. Supra-nationalism will come, because it must; but the great chance will have been lost of bringing it in from the first under Socialist auspices and in a Socialist form.

CHAPTER XIII

GERMANY IN THE NEW EUROPE

GREAT BRITAIN, as the sole West European Power which has survived the Nazi onslaught, has become the asylum of every sort of exile from the countries that have been overrun. London is the temporary meeting-place of politicians of every shade of opinion from reactionary legitimism to Socialism, the temporary seat of exiled Governments of varying political composition, the centre for all manner of schemes for giving every colour of the rainbow to the post-war settlement of Europe. Crowned heads, with their depleted courts, and heads uncrowned since the last war, are in our midst, scheming and intriguing for a future which will restore them to dignity and affluence.

Politicians of a wide variety of views, bankers and business men, and sheer adventurers go about seeking British sympathisers for their several designs. Among them are the erstwhile leaders—or rather such of them as have been able to escape—of the Social Democratic and Labour Parties of the occupied countries, together with a sprinkling of Trade Union officials—all alike cut off from their former followers, and knowing but little of what is going on in the minds of their countrymen, whom they have left behind to endure the Nazi occupation.

All these are leaders, almost without followers; for hardly any of the followers were able to escape. The reactionaries are, for the most part, in a much better position than the Socialists or even the 'Liberals' for keeping touch with their own countries. For they have many more friends who have come to terms with the conquerors, or are living, practically unpersecuted, under their rule. The Socialists, on the other hand, except the few renegades who have gone over to the Nazi side, are enduring systematic persecution. The leaders who did not escape, and many of their most active followers, are dead or in concentration camps; and those active Socialists and Trade Unionists who are still at large live under continuous danger of delation and arrest. Some of them, bravely, carry on with underground propaganda, and take great risks in order both to keep the spirit of revolt alive and to maintain some sort of contact with their exiled comrades.

How big, or how successful, these underground movements are it is exceedingly difficult to tell. The groups carrying them on must be small and largely isolated one from another; and even so the loss of active workers by discovery and arrest is bound to be very heavy. Hardest of all is it to know how underground work is faring in Germany itself; for there the Gestapo has had long practice in the arts of detection, and the interruption of communications has been more complete than elsewhere.

Yet it is of vital importance for the exiles now in Great Britain to keep in constant touch with the anti-Nazi elements in their own countries. The position of exiled leaders is bound to be precarious; for they may easily cease to understand what is passing in the minds of those who were their followers, and therefore become powerless to influence them, or to resume their place in leadership when and if the chance comes. At present, this danger is greatest of all in the case of the exiles from Germany, not only because contacts are harder to maintain, but even more because the Social Democratic leadership of pre-Nazi Germany can by no means evade a serious part of the blame for Hitler's victory. It may be that the Social Democrats of other countries would have put up as poor a show if they had been faced with the same difficulties. Indeed, the French Socialists did not come off much better in their day of trial. But the fact remains that the German Social Democrats did show a sorry want of resolution in their handling of the Nazi peril, and that upon them rests, in the minds of German people, the stigma of ignominious failure.

I am not going to argue here how far the folly of the Communists was responsible for this failure, by disrupting the Socialist forces in Germany and sapping the will-power of the Socialist and Trade Union leadership. I am not trying to apportion blame, but only to state facts. It is a fact that the old German Social Democracy (not the Austrian, for the Austrians did fight, though not with all their strength) is discredited as well as defeated, and that the German people, even when they weary of the Nazis, are most unlikely to look for new leadership to the old leaders of the defeated Social Democratic Party.

If and when German Socialism rises again, it will be new-born, and not a mere continuation of the former Social Democratic tradition. The fault of this tradition, both politically and industrially—for the same vice infected the Trade Unions—was that of over-centralisation and bureaucracy. On paper, both the Party and the Trade Unions were magnificently organised; and they did in fact a great deal of excellent work. But they allowed altogether too little scope for personal or group initiative; and they suffered from over-rationalisation—from a delusion that making plans was the same thing as acting on them, and wishing the good the same thing as willing it with all their powers. Consequently, they created a docile, instead of a militant, movement; and when the time of trial came, the leaders quibbled about legality, and the followers, left without fighting leadership, lacked the initiative, save in a few places, to take matters into their own hands.

It is sometimes argued that this docility is an essential part of the German character. But this is not so, in any sense which prevents the growth of actively militant movements, or Hitler would never have succeeded in building up his very active following among the German youth. It is, I think, true that the Germans love system and order and take readily to dogmas which purport to explain everything in terms of some one infallible master idea. But that is quite another thing, fully consistent with active militancy, though not so fully consistent with democracy, in the sense in which it is understood in Great Britain and over the rest of Western Europe. The German attitude was fully compatible with the growth of a powerful Communist Party, which might have been much more powerful if it had been more wisely led. I am not so sure that it was in the long run compatible with the type of Social Democracy which had developed in Germany under the old *Reich*, and came under the test of practical capacity when power was thrust into its hands with the establishment of the Weimar Republic.

For it can hardly be denied that the Social Democrats made a great mess of their opportunities. Be it admitted that they had great difficulties to face. Their first necessity was to feed a starving people, and they had reason to fear that any sign of 'Bolshevism' on their part might call down on them the vengeance of the Allies in the form of a blockade. Be it admitted that, in the critical days and weeks after the Armistice, this fear helped to paralyse their action. The fact remains that at no time between the German Revolution of 1918 and the victory of Hitler did the Social Democrats make any real effort to establish Socialism. They used reactionary corps of ex-officers to repress extremist movements among the workers: they allowed the Reichswehr to become a rallying point for the old militarist and aristocratic elements in German society; and they failed to press on with any really Socialist programme even when the risk of Allied action against them had altogether ceased to be serious. Consequently, whereas at the foundation of the Weimar Republic it seemed as if nothing could stand in the way of the reconstruction of German society on a basis at any rate largely Socialist, gradually the people lost faith in both Socialism and the parliamentary democracy which the Socialists accepted, and there was a drift away to Communism on the one hand and to Nazism on the other. In many cases the disillusioned workers turned first to Communism and then, disillusioned again, to Nazism, because first one and then the other seemed, as Social Democracy did not, to offer some hope of escape from a very depressing situation, and some active work for them to do. At the time of the Kapp *Putsch* Social Democracy did no doubt assert itself powerfully as a negative force; but it never managed to convert its negative opposition to the *Putsch* into an active programme of Socialist construction. It seemed as if the parliamentarism which the Social Democrats professed was continually paralysing their powers of action, and as if their leaders, like the people at large, regarded the Weimar Republic, not as an instrument of creation, but rather as a melancholy necessity. German parliamentarism remained both uninspiring and uninspired; and it was difficult not to associate its weakness with an unfitness of the parliamentary form, as the Germans used it, for the pursuance of bold or far-reaching policies of social change. The consequences were that the parliamentary-democratic form of government came to be associated in the minds of many Germans, not only with the humiliation of national defeat, but also with the persistence of depression and confusion in the situation of the country, and that Social Democracy lost caste because it seemed to have so thoroughly identified itself with a system that could not be made to work.

This is another way of saying that I am not at all sure whether democratic parliamentarism can be a suitable form of government for Germany, at all events for a considerable time to come. For parliamentary government implies both a large element of give and take, and a considerable tolerance of untidiness and illogicality. Where there is a strong opposition, with a full right to speak its mind and to organise public opinion, the Government hardly ever gets its way completely. Politics are an affair of part-achievements, of sacrificing this in order to get that, of doing things a different way round in order to disarm or circumvent opposition. The workability of this form of government depends not only on the existence of a strong feeling of community in a people, underlying political differences, but also on a belief in the virtue of arguing things out, and doing by consent whatever can be so done. The Germans possess very strongly the sense of community; but this sense has been apt, consciously from the time of Hegel, and unconsciously a great deal earlier, to take the form of a belief that the whole German people ought to be made to do the same thing, and that difference of conduct or opinion is a form of disloyalty or treason to the national spirit.

Now, the German Social Democrats were, from the very beginning of their success as a parliamentary party, in an anomalous position. Their political theory was Marxist, and permeated by the idea of unity in true German fashion. But their political practice was modelled on the—chiefly

British—tradition of parliamentary action as a continuous process of give and take. It was not the British Labour Party they imitated—it was hardly there to be imitated when German Social Democracy assumed its characteristic forms. Their imitation was of the British parliamentary tradition; and it did not fit in at all well with their theory, based on revolutionary Marxism. This was the inwardness of the famous 'Revisionist' controversy in the German Socialist movement early in the present century. The Revisionists, headed by Bernstein, who knew England well, wanted to amend the theory to fit the practice. Bernstein was denounced as a renegade from Marxism; and the party preferred to carry on with the misfit rather than give up either its 'all-or-nothing' theory or its 'give-and-take' practice.

It did this, I am convinced, because it was aware, deep down in its consciousness, that the practice to which it was committed did not express its real mind. It was totalitarian in its basic attitude, as the Russian Communists were, though its current practice was that of Western liberalism. Germany, altogether, and not only German Socialism, suffered from this divided mind. The Germans tried to go thoroughly 'liberal' after 1918. But they were half-hearted and half-minded about it—Socialists and all. The Weimar Republic, being 'liberal' in conception, did not fit the German idea. Communism might have fitted it, but would have involved a sharp break with the West. Communism therefore grew strong enough to undermine Social Democracy, but not to conquer the country. Nazism came afterwards and picked up the pieces.

Even if I am wrong in this retrospective view of German Socialism, there is another, much more obvious, reason for doubting the likelihood of an easy return in Germany to a 'liberal' system of government. No country can pass through an experience such as Germany has suffered of late without emerging scarred and altered. It is simply not possible that, upon the overthrow of the Nazis, the German

people can settle down to live quietly together, Nazis and
anti-Nazis, forming an amiable society, with the horrors
of the concentration camps forgotten or overlooked. There
will be too many people who will remember the torture
and murder of their friends and relations, to say nothing of
their personal sufferings, and, on the other side, too many,
brought up in the savage cult of Nazism, who will hanker
after the lost opportunities for sadism and brutality. A
country in such a pathological condition will inevitably
need strong government until there has been time for the
wounds to heal. One notion, widely entertained in certain
quarters, is that this strong government should be provided
by a foreign army of occupation. But, apart from the
question of expediency, what likelihood is there that either
Great Britain or the United States or the Soviet Union
would consent to garrison and govern a defeated Germany
for an indefinite term of years? And, on the question of
expediency, would such a method be likely to accelerate, or
to defer, the growing together again of the Germans as a
people able to live in peace and harmony? Some garrisoning there may have to be, whether the countries which are
called upon to do it like it or not. But that can be only a
very temporary measure at most; and, in any event,
garrisoning and governing are different things. Post-war
Germany will have to govern itself; and I suggest that its
immediate government is most unlikely to take an orthodox
'liberal' parliamentary form.

I am sure these considerations are important in relation
to the part which Germany is destined to play in the post-
war re-settlement of Europe. If I am even broadly right,
it is of no use to expect the Germans, for a considerable time
after the war, if at all, to settle down comfortably inside a
supra-national West European State based on the 'liberal'
parliamentary tradition. If they were to be made part of
such a State on the morrow of defeat, they would not merely
be half-hearted about it, as they were about the Weimar

Republic. They would find its institutions altogether unworkable in face of the current temper of political opinion. They would need a stronger hand over them, in Germany itself, to prevent them from coming to blows. A 'liberal' Republic, even on a Socialist basis, would not suit the immediate conditions. I am even doubtful whether such a Republic is consistent at all with the 'all-or-nothing' tendency of the German, or at least the Prussian, mind.

I am fully aware that what I am saying is likely to annoy many Germans almost as much as they are annoyed by Lord Vansittart's foolish tirades. I cannot help that: I have to say what I think, because it is of vital importance for us all not to indulge in wish-fulfilments, but to consider clearly and hard-headedly what can, and what cannot, be expected of post-war Germany. The reason why many of my German friends will be annoyed with me is that they, being personally 'liberals' and setting great store by the values of Western 'liberal' culture, passionately want Germany to come back into the stream of the West European 'liberal' tradition, of which they see Social Democracy as the only logical continuation under the conditions of the present time. When I suggest that perhaps the German people does not fully share their enlightened outlook, and has in any case been driven into a state of neurosis which it will take a long time to cure, they are angry with me, and accuse me of regarding the Germans as a pack of barbarians, and forgetting the truly immense contributions which Germans have made to the common culture of the West.

Well, of course the Germans are not barbarians. They were, until very lately, a group of peoples second to none in their achievements in the arts, the sciences, and the practical techniques of economic organisation. Western culture and Western science are, at the moment, alike the poorer for their recent estrangement. But therewith goes a contradiction. Many Germans have been great 'liberals', and doubtless many are. But Germany, as a political entity, has never accepted 'liberalism'. Many Germans are as good 'liberal' Socialists as I am; but it does not follow that Germany is capable of becoming a 'liberal' Socialist Republic. Saxony might, or some of the other German lands. Austria might. But could Prussia? Or could Germany as a whole, if Prussia could not?

The Germans, in effect, have never had their 'liberal' revolution. They failed to achieve it in 1848, and in 1918 they failed to hold it. I very much doubt whether they can have it at the end of this war, after so many happenings that have sapped the vitality of the 'liberal' spirit. And it is even possible that they could never have had it in any real sense. It looks now as if the coming German Revolution will have to be a Communist, or at any rate a Soviet, Revolution, and as if the place of Germany in the new Europe will be nearer to the Soviet Union than to Great Britain.

Such an idea is bound to be the more annoying to many German Social Democrats because the very weakness of the liberal spirit in Germany makes them the more desirous of linking their country with the West, in order to strengthen the liberal tendencies within it. The very reaction against Nazism is in their minds a reaction towards Western morality, and against totalitarianism in all its forms. They have had ample cause to hate the Communist Party, and are in any case disposed to regard the Russians as the barbarians, and themselves as standing in the forefront of the European cultural tradition. Surely it is for the Russians to go on learning from them, not for them to learn from Russia. I sympathise keenly with this feeling; but I cannot base much hope upon it. What I am afraid of is that it will lead the exiled Social Democrats of Germany very far away from the sentiments of their own countrymen, including those who are destined to be in the forefront of the German rebellion against the Nazi spirit.

We have seen in earlier chapters that, from the economic point of view, it is right for Germany to be closely associated with the less developed areas of Southern and Eastern Europe. Germany is the natural market for much of the produce of these areas; and German industry is in the best position, by way of exchange, to foster their economic development. Under the Nazis, this process of exchange becomes one of exploitation. But there is no reason why it should be so under a different German régime. A plan for Central and Eastern Europe, based on the use of German technical skill and economic resources in developing the more backward areas, is plain commonsense, if only it can be carried through on terms fair to all the parties.

It is very doubtful whether the backward countries of Eastern and Southern Europe are suitable for parliamentary government. Some sort of Soviet system may suit their needs much better, as it has undoubtedly suited the Russians. May not this be true of Germany also, in view of what has happened there in recent years? May not the best available solution for Central as well as for Eastern Europe be a Soviet Revolution, leading on to the creation of a second Union of Soviet Republics stretching alongside the U.S.S.R., from the Baltic to the Mediterranean? May it not even be better, if this solution does not prove practicable, for Germany, as well as Eastern Europe, to be included in an enlarged U.S.S.R.?

I am not being dogmatic about this. I realise that I may be quite wrong about it, and that the Germans themselves may prove me wrong. If so, I shall be very far from feeling any regrets. It is for the Germans, in making their revolution against Hitler, to decide whether they can best adopt a Soviet or a parliamentary system, or link their fortunes more closely with the 'liberal' West or the totalitarian East. If I have a fancy that they—that is, the people now in Germany, with whom the real decision will rest—are likely to prefer totalitarianism to 'liberal' Socialism, that is not because I want them to do so—for I dislike totalitarianism in all its forms—but because I have a feeling that another attempt to establish 'liberal' Socialism in Germany will be terribly likely to go the way of the Weimar Republic.

Indeed, I believe the Germans are by temperament much more totalitarian than the Russians. I have said earlier that the Bolshevik Revolution in Russia was an essay in westernisation—an attempt to impose on the backward Russian peoples a part of the tradition of the West. But the part which was thus imposed was much more German than French or British. It was German Marxism applied to the conditions of the autocratic Czarist Empire. The Russians, so far from showing by nature the German love of method and order, have in them a strongly anarchist tendency, which has been rigorously suppressed ever since the Bolsheviks broke with the Left Social Revolutionaries—their partners in the original Soviet Government. This tendency will reassert itself when the revolutionary crisis ends and the country is able to settle down to steady development. It is the basis on which a return to diversity will be made, the rigid discipline of the revolution broken, and foundations for the growth of cultural liberalism laid.

The Germans, on the other hand, are almost entirely devoid of natural anarchism. Syndicalism and the movements related to it made almost no appeal in Germany, when they were sweeping over most of Europe. If the Germans adopt Soviet Communism as a means of overthrowing Hitlerism and building their new State, they will be very thorough about it—more thorough than the Russians—terribly thorough in many ways.

I do not want this to happen. I want it not to happen. I want the German Revolution to take a form which will bring the new German Republic into the family of Western nations, and make possible a full association between Germans, French, British, Scandinavians, and all the other groups which could work fruitfully together in creating the new Europe—if only they could agree not merely on a common set of institutions, but also on a common way of regarding them. But, frankly, I doubt the possibility of this happening, at any rate in the near future; and Europe cannot afford another Weimar fiasco, or another war.

The vital thing is to make sure of successful revolution in Germany—successful Socialist Revolution. In comparison, it matters much less what form that revolution takes—whether 'liberal' or totalitarian. For, unless Germany can be won for Socialism, of some sort, I do not see how Europe is to be saved from an early recurrence of war. Therefore, it seems to me, the only suitable policy is to concentrate on bringing about in Germany that type of revolution which has the best chance of success; and, realising that I may be mistaken, I feel, on such evidence as I possess, that working for a Soviet Revolution offers greater promise of success than working for a 'liberal' revolution based on the Social Democratic tradition.

If my German friends in this country disagree with this view, I will only ask them not to be too sure, and not to close the door to the alternative. Immediately, what this means is that it is important for German Socialists to put as far as possible out of their minds their old causes of quarrel with the Communist Party of Germany and with the Soviet Union, and to do their utmost to come to an agreement with the Soviet leaders about the methods which are to be used in preparing the way for the German revolution. For, if the Russians try to bring about one kind of revolution and the exiles here another, and if the old divisions between German Communists and German Social Democrats are perpetuated and made the basis of new feuds, how is it possible to hope that fruitful work can be done? When the time comes, it will be for the people of Germany to settle the shape of their new society, and the nature of its affiliations to the rest of Europe. But in the meantime it is the task of Socialists to do their utmost to bring the German revolution about; and that will assuredly not be done if Communists continue to denounce Social

Democrats and Social Democrats Communists as enemies of the people, and if no agreement is reached whereby the Soviet Union and the Western countries can work together on the basis of a common propaganda directed to the German people as a whole. The divided counsels of Communists and Social Democrats, however easily explained in the light of the past, are grist to Hitler's mill: nor have they any relation to the real problems of contemporary Germany. For only by uniting all the anti-Nazi forces in Germany can the way to successful revolution be made open. The task will be hard enough, even so: it will be impossible if German Communists and German Social Democrats continue fighting one another, and German exiles here push one sort of German revolution, while the Soviet Union works quite independently for a revolution of a different kind.

CHAPTER XIV

THE ESSENTIALS OF DEMOCRACY

I AM WRITING this book as a Socialist of many years' standing. During those years I have passed through many happenings which have caused me to change my mind about this or that particular doctrine, or about the relative emphasis to be laid on different elements of my Socialist faith. But not one of these happenings has given me reason for believing that my fundamental approach has been wrong, or made me less a Socialist than I was in the first flush of my political awakening, more than a third of a century ago.

Let me try, by way of conclusion to the argument of this book, to restate the fundamental reasons which make me a Socialist. I believe that social institutions have two, and only two, legitimate purposes—to ensure to men the supply of the material means of good living, and to give men the fullest possible scope for creative activity. It is conceivable that these two purposes—or rather the means of pursuing them—may clash; for example, if higher production requires from men a subordination to routine processes which leaves no room for the sense of creative freedom. Where such clashes do arise, compromises have to be made. Men have to choose between their desire as consumers for a higher standard of material living and their desire as producers for a less irksome way of life. The best set of social institutions is that which finds the best compromise available under the prevailing conditions.

Who, then, is to settle what is best? Who, but the whole people, who must endure for good or ill the consequences of the decision? If the good life is a blend of satisfactions achieved from consumption and satisfactions achieved from successful creation, the only answer I find tolerable is that men themselves must decide collectively what blending of these elements they like best.

I am thus led to a belief in democracy by two routes. I believe in democracy because I believe that every citizen has a right to play a part in deciding how society can best be organised in the cause of human happiness, and also because democracy is itself one of the fundamental exercises of free creative activity. It follows that I mean by democracy not merely the right of a majority to have its way, but an arrangement of public affairs which is designed to give every man and woman the best possible chance of finding out what they really want, of persuading others to accept their point of view, and of playing an active part in the working of a system thus responsive to their needs. Not that, under any system, most people will take a continuous active interest in public affairs : not at all. But everyone ought to have a fair chance of taking an interest in them and of carrying some weight if he does take an interest. This too I am sure about—that a society, whatever its formal structure, *cannot* be democratic unless a goodly number of men and women do take an interest in making and keeping it so.

F

That is my idea of democracy. It involves many other things—free speech, freedom of organisation, freedom to develop the personality in diverse ways. It cannot mean any of these things without limit—for society in itself implies limits—but it means that the limits must be very wide. My idea of democracy excludes a regimented society, an indoctrinated society, a society in which men are not allowed to organise freely for all sorts of purposes without any interference by the police, a society in which it is supposed to be a virtue for everybody to think like his neighbours. My idea of democracy excludes too much tidiness, too much order, too much having everything taped. I believe every good democrat is a bit of an anarchist when he's scratched.

Next point. My notion of democracy is that it involves a sense of comradeship, friendliness, brotherhood—call it what you like. I mean a warm sense—not a mere recognition, cold as a fish. I mean that democracy means loving your neighbours, or at any rate being ready to love them when you don't happen to dislike them too much—and even then, when they're in trouble, and come after you, looking for help and sympathy. A democrat is someone who has a physical glow of sympathy and love for anyone who comes to him, honestly, looking for help or sympathy: a man isn't a democrat, however justly he may try to behave to his fellow man, unless he feels like that. But—and here's the point—you can't feel that glow about people—individual people, with capacities for doing and suffering—unless and until you know them personally. And you can't know, personally, more than a quite small number of people.

That is why real democracies have either to be small, or to be broken up into small, human groups in which men and women can know and love one another. If human societies get too big, and are not broken up in that way, the human spirit goes out of them; and the spirit of democracy goes out too. What walks in instead is demagogy—a very different thing. Men feel lonely in a great crowd unless there is someone to hustle them into herd activity. In their loneliness they follow the man with the loudest voice, or in these days, the loudest loud-speaker and the most efficient propagandist technique. They suck in mass-produced ideas as a substitute for having ideas of their own: they all shout in unison because they have no one to talk to quietly—no group to go about with, no little world of a few people in which they can count as individuals and work out lives of their own. You can have various kinds of society under these conditions. You can have Fascism, or you can have what the Fascists call plutodemocracy. You can even have Communism, of a perverted sort. But you can't have democracy. For democracy means a society in which everyone has a chance to count as an individual, and to do something that is distinctively his own.

Rousseau, knowing all this, thought that democracy could exist only in small States. The revolutionary philosophers who followed him thought they had solved the problem of having democracy in large States by the simple device of representation, whereby one man could represent and stand for many men in public affairs. But one man can't stand for many men, or for anybody except himself. That was where the nineteenth-century democrats went wrong, mistaking parliamentarism and representative local government for instruments of democracy, which they plainly are not. If you think they are, ask the man in the street—any ordinary man who isn't much of a politician, what he thinks. He doesn't think Parliament is democratic—even when it is elected by all the people—not a bit of it; and he is right. One man can't represent another—that's flat. The odd thing is that anyone should ever have supposed he could.

So, as States get bigger, and the representative gets further off the people he is supposed to represent, till most of his constituents don't know him, most have never seen him, and quite a number can't even tell you his name, what democracy there was dies out of the machinery of government. For what democracy there was—and there was never very much—depended much less on the fact that people elected their M.P. than on their knowing him personally, knowing about him, what he did and how he behaved, who his father and mother were, and his cousins and his friends, how he got on with his wife, and all the rest of the things people know about one another in a village, but don't know in a big town. Villages are more democratic places than towns, even when they vote as the squire and the parson tell them. Being democratic isn't the same thing as holding advanced opinions. It isn't the same thing as believing in democracy. It starts with knowing your neighbours as real persons; and unless it starts there, it doesn't start at all.

Of course, knowing your neighbours as real persons isn't democracy, any more than a steel ingot is a battleship, or even part of one. But this sort of knowing is part of the material out of which democracy has to be built. You can't build democracy without it. That is what has gone wrong with our modern democratic societies. All the time we have been broadening the franchise, and increasing educational opportunities, and developing the social services, and all the rest of it, we have been letting the very essence of democracy get squeezed out by the mere growth in the scale of political organisation. It is even true that each successive widening of the franchise has made our system less really democratic, by making the relation between electors and elected more and more unreal.

Men, being men, don't lie down quite tamely under this deprivation of democracy. They keep what they can of it by making, within the great societies, little societies of their own. They form little social groups of friends, or of persons drawn together by a common friendlessness—*clubs des sans club*. They organise for all sorts of purposes—recreative, instructive, reformative, revolutionary, religious, economic, or just social—in associations and groups of all sizes. But when these groups get big the same nemesis overtakes them as overtakes the political machine. Their natural democracy evaporates and bureaucracy steps into its place. You can see this happening to the Trade Unions, which are a great deal less democratic when they have grown into huge national associations than they were when they were simply little local Trade Clubs meeting in an inn or a coffee house, so that each member knew each other personally.

Such little groups exist still—any number of them. But the growth in the scale of living drives them out of public influence. There are fewer and fewer important jobs for them to do, except in the purely social sphere. There they remain immensely important, rescuing countless souls from the torment of loneliness and despair. But they don't, in rescuing these souls, play any part in the more public affairs of society. They don't affect political or economic policies, or give any democratic character to men's behaviour in their collective concerns. As a consequence, men's public and private lives slip further and further apart; and not only artists and other exceptional people, but quite ordinary men and women, get to despising politics in their hearts, and to saying openly that politics is a rotten game, and thinking of politics as something it won't help them to bother their heads about: so they had better not. Politics for the politicians! The last corruption of a democracy that has knocked the foundations from under its own feet.

In such a society, politics *is* a rotten game. It is bound to be; for it has no roots in the real lives of the people. It is either a vast makebelieve or, behind its pretences, a sordid affair of vested interests. In terms of vital ideas, or of common living to the glory of God, or of the City, or of the spirit of man, it doesn't mean a thing. It has therefore neither imagination to create the means to the good life nor power to defend itself against any vital new force, good or evil, that challenges its supremacy.

Fortunately, there are in the countries which live under parliamentary institutions other elements of democracy which are not so defenceless. The real democracy that does exist in Great Britain, for example, is to be found for the most part not in Parliament or in the institutions of local government, but in the smaller groups, formal or informal, in which men and women join together out of decent fellowship or for the pursuit of a common social purpose—societies, clubs, churches, and not least informal neighbourhood groups. It is in these fellowships, and in the capacity to form them swiftly under the pressure of immediate needs, that the real spirit of democracy resides. It was by virtue of this capacity that the workers in the factories responded so remarkably to the urgent need that followed upon the fall of France, and that, a few months later, the whole people of many great cities found courage to resist the impact of intensive air bombardment. The tradition of British democracy, which goes back above all to seventeenth-century Puritanism, reasserted itself strongly in spite of the immensely powerful forces which have been sapping its foundations in recent years.

This tradition is still powerful, deep down in the consciousness of the people. Moreover, it blends with another tradition, on the surface antagonistic to it, and going much further back in the history of this country. This is the Christian ethic and the tradition of Christianity as a social force impregnating every social activity with a moral purpose. The spirit underlying mediaeval gild organisation, not only in the economic sphere but also in many others, was within its limited range a true spirit of human brotherhood, the more intense because the groups through which it found expression were small and neighbourly. That kind of organisation (which, of course, touched the countryside only to a small extent) died out under the combined impact of economic revolution and religious reformation. Merchants intent on breaking down parochial restrictions in order to widen the market collaborated in destroying it with Puritans intent on establishing direct relations between man and his

God without the mediation of Mother Church. Economics and religion set sail together for the El Dorado of individualism, taking away from men the small groups in which the older social tradition, now grown too cramping in face of the development of new knowledge, had been incorporated, and leaving the ordinary man lonelier and more afraid in a world too big for him to master or to find his way in.

That, however, was just where Puritanism, transformed into Nonconformity, was able to reassert itself as a corrective force. The traders and industrialists got their way, and converted the economic terrain into a hedgeless and fenceless open country of competitive enterprise. The religious reformers were much less thoroughly successful because the traders, having won their economic victory, ceased to battle on their side. Lutheranism came to terms with the new Nation State, and converted itself in secular matters into its obedient instrument, saving only its right to go on, otherworldly, with its business of saving souls from the everlasting fire. Calvinism, on the other hand, after a brief reign of theocracy in a few places, became a focus of opposition to the new order, as it had been to the old. Barely tolerated in most countries, and seldom given any recognition, it was compelled in self-defence to organise itself democratically in small, self-governing congregations. It became in this way the great school of democracy—the only, or almost the only, repository of the true democratic values until, with the advent of steam-power and the factory system, working-class organisation began to develop on a basis of small-scale, neighbourhood groups of craftsmen subject to a common exploitation and conscious of common rights.

Opposition and persecution are great levellers, and therefore great teachers of democracy. Success and recognition, on the other hand, are very apt to kill the democratic spirit. This is not only because, having won something, men grow less enthusiastic for what remains to be won. It is even more because success and recognition enlarge the scale of organisation, cause it to become more centralised, and diminish the importance of local leadership, local initiative, and the individual contribution of every member. Every large organisation that is able to administer its affairs openly without let or hindrance develops bureaucratic tendencies. It becomes officialised—even official-ridden: its rank and file members come to feel less responsibility for its doings. The spirit of sacrifice and of brotherhood grows weaker in it. Its tasks come to be regarded as falling upon those who are paid for doing them: the duty of the member comes to be regarded as one mainly of acquiescence in the official decisions. In a persecuted body, on the other hand, and to a great extent in one which is prevented from any cause from becoming centralised, each member is under a continual pressure to be up and doing. There must be, in every group, close and constant consultation upon policy, a constant sharing-out of tasks, a constant willingness to help one another—or, in other words, the spirit of democracy must be continually invoked.

Does this mean that democracy is, in sober truth, only a by-product of persecution and intolerance? These evil forces have, there can be no doubt, been vastly important in creating the democratic spirit. It is to be hoped they are at work, re-creating it to-day, all over Europe. But we need not conclude that democracies are always fated to perish in the hour of victory, unless we also conclude that it is beyond men's power to stand out against the forces which impel societies towards bureaucratic centralisation. If indeed bureaucracy is the unavoidable accompaniment of all large-scale organisation—I mean, bureaucracy as its dominant force and characteristic—the game is up. But need this be?

It will be, unless men are vigilantly on their guard against it. For both increasing population, with its accompaniment of increasing concentration in large groups, and the increasing scale of production make for bureaucracy. These forces destroy remorselessly the natural small units of earlier days

—the village or little town, the group of workmates in a workshop or small factory, the personal acquaintance that crosses the barriers of class and calling. They convert the factory into a huge establishment in which it is impossible for everyone to know everyone else, the town into a huge agglomeration of strangers. They compel men to travel long distances to and from work, and therefore to scurry away from the factory as soon as the day's work is done, without building up close social contacts with their fellow-workers. At the other end, they send men scurrying from home, which becomes more and more a dormitory rather than the centre of a common life. The city develops its amusement zone, where strangers jostle; and if a man stays in his own place, the wireless ensures that a large part of his recreation shall isolate him from, instead of uniting him with, his neighbours.

There are, superficially, many conveniences in the new ways of living. So many that we may take it for granted men will never willingly give them up. Indeed, why should they, when almost every one of them, taken by itself, is a gain? For the disadvantage lies not in the technical changes themselves, but in men's failure to square up to the new problems of successful living which they involve. The disadvantage is intangible, and not easily seen (though it is experienced) by the individual who is unused to taking general views. The man or woman who has less and less intimate knowledge of his neighbours, less and less intense participation in any small social group to which he feels an obligation, a less and less integrated and purposeful life, and less and less sense of responsibility for his fellows, does not, unless he is a bit of a philosopher, inquire why these things have happened. He may indeed be unconscious that they have happened, and conscious merely of a vague and un-identified emptiness in his way of living. But even so, if I am right in believing that the void is there, he will be very ready to respond to anyone who will offer him the means of filling it up.

He will respond, for good or for evil. He will be ready to

F 2

join an anti-social 'gang', if no one offers him anything else. He will respond to any mass-propaganda that blares loudly enough at him with a message of comradeship. He will rally to Dr. Buchman, or to Sir Oswald Mosley, rather than not rally at all, when once he has become acutely aware of his own *malaise*. He wants comrades, even if they be comrades in enmity against something to which he has, at bottom, no real objection. He wants comrades, and the society he lives in offers him only a scurvying loneliness among the scurvying hosts of strangers.

This desire for comradeship is the stuff out of which we must build democracy, if we are to build it at all. Build it and preserve it—that is what we must do. And this means that, in this age of hugeness, we must still find means of resting our society on a foundation of small groups, of giving these small groups a functional place in our society, of integrating them with the larger organisations which are indispensable for modern living, of encouraging a continual development of new groups responding to developing needs, and, last but not least, of countering every tendency towards bureaucratisation of this quintessential group life.

How can we rest a society as huge as ours on a secure foundation of small, intensively democratic groupings? This society of ours is based of necessity on large-scale production: it involves, at any rate for a long time to come, the existence of huge cities; and it is in need, in many respects, of even huger organisation on a supra-national scale—for the prevention of war, for example, and for the fuller development of international trade and exchange. We cannot turn our backs on these forces: we have to accept them because they are to-day as much a part of the given environment as sea and land, mountains and river-valleys, heat and cold, and all the other things which form part of our natural environment. The task before us is not analogous to that of draining the ocean; but it is analogous to that great victory of man which turned the ocean, heretofore a barrier, into a means of communication between land and land. We have to turn the very hugeness of the modern world into a means for the higher expression of the human spirit.

We cannot do this by changing man's stature; for man remains little, and is destined so to remain always. The Superman is a vain notion; and 'Back to Methuselah' is another. Mark Twain once wrote that if it were possible to educate a flea up to the size of a man, that flea would be President of the United States. It is not possible to inflate humanity up to the size of the organisations it has made. But it is possible so to arrange our affairs that little men are not merely lost in a world too big and directionless for them to find their way.

Men's easiest ways of grouping are round the places they live in and the places they work in. These are two bases of natural human relationship which can be used as bases for democracy. Take the factory. It is not enough for factory workers to belong to a Trade Union, which will represent them in negotiations about wages, hours of labour, and general working conditions throughout their trade. The Trade Union, under modern conditions, is necessarily much too remote from their working lives. Even if it is broken up into branches, these seldom coincide with the personnel of a particular factory or workshop, and are as a rule much more concerned with matters of national policy than with immediate workshop affairs. Side by side with the Trade Union, and perhaps wholly independent of it, there needs to be a workshop group, consisting of all the workers in a particular shop, irrespective of their trade or degree of skill. This group ought to have a recognised right of meeting on the factory premises, its own chosen leaders, and—here is the main point—a right to discuss and resolve upon anything under the sun, from the conduct of a particular manager or foreman to the policy of the national Cabinet, or anything else about which its members happen to feel strongly.

Observe that I say 'workshop group', and not 'factory

group'. In the case of small establishments, the factory may serve as a unit; but the large factory is much too big to function as a primary neighbourhood group, or to have in it the essential quality of basic democracy. The shop stewards' movement that grew up between 1915 and 1918 was feeling after just this basic democracy. But it always found the Trade Union bureaucracy against it, because it seemed to, and did, stand for an alternative basis of social organisation. It was truly democratic; and accordingly the bureaucrats were eager to knock it on the head. They did not object to shop stewards who kept to their proper functions—that is, acted merely as subordinate agents of the Trade Union machine. They objected strongly to a shop stewards' movement which laid claim to any independent initiative or showed signs of assuming a 'political' character.

Consider now the places in which people live. Here in my mind's eye is a street of houses—or rather several streets. This one, a row of nineteenth-century working-class dwellings, all joined on, short of light and air and comfort and even of elementary requirements. This other, a street on a post-war housing estate, immensely superior in lay-out and amenity and capacity to afford the environmental conditions of healthy living. This again, a street of shops, and this, not exactly a street, but a great block of flats housing more people than many streets.

What is odd about these places? The oddest thing, to my mind, is that the people who live in them, though they are neighbours with a multitude of common problems, hardly ever meet in conclave to consider these problems, and have in hardly any instance any sort of common organisation. It is true that the shopkeepers may just possibly have some rudimentary association among themselves—but even that is unlikely. It is true that, here and there, struggles between landlords and householders have brought into being some sort of Tenants' League, for a narrow range of purposes. But in the vast majority of streets there is not even the shadow of a social unity, joining these people together on the basis of their common neighbourhood.

A second thing, not so odd but well worth noting, is that of these bodies of street-dwellers those who know one another best are pretty certain to be those who are living under the worst housing conditions. There is a comradeship of the street in a poor working-class quarter: there is usually much less on the model housing estate or in the model block of flats.

I am suggesting that there ought to be for every street, or little group of streets, for every block of flats, and of course for every village and hamlet a regularly meeting, recognised neighbourhood group, with a right to discuss and resolve upon anything under the sun. I am not merely suggesting that this ought to happen: I say it ought to be made to happen. Every new group of streets we build ought to have its little Moot Hall for such assemblies of its people, ought to have its little centre for their communal affairs. Personally, I think this Moot Hall should be also a communal restaurant and bakehouse, and a social club. I think it should include a place where children could amuse themselves, and be left in charge of somebody when their parents are away. I think, as we rebuild our cities, there should be open space round these centres—space for games, for sitting about, for children's playing. I think we should make our Community Centres, not merely one to a big housing estate, but one to every street, or group of streets, of say a hundred or at most a few hundred households.

But to enlarge on all this would take me too far from my immediate purpose. Whether these other things are done or not done, I am sure there must be really active neighbourhood groups in every street and village before we can call our country truly a democracy. One reason for this is that there is no other way of bringing the ordinary housewife right into politics without interfering with her duties as housewife and mother. Workshop organisation may come first in the minds of the men and young women who work in factories: neighbourhood groups are the key to the active citizenship of the wife and mother.

It is of no use to think that we can have these groups and confine their activities to the specific affairs of the little places to which they are directly attached. They must and will deal with these affairs, and they should be given a positive and assured status in dealing with them. But this is not their sole, or even their main purpose. They are wanted most of all to serve as basic and natural units of democracy in a world ridden by large-scale organisation. Their task is one of democratic education and awakening—of ensuring democratic vigilance through the length and breadth of the great society. Therefore they must be free, like the workshop Soviets, to discuss and resolve upon what they will.

Soviets—I have used the word at last. Soviets, as they arose all over Russia on the morrow of the revolution. Soviets, expressing directly the common attitude of small groups in any important relation of life. To what extent such Soviets are effective to-day in the Soviet Union I do not fully know; but I believe them to be much more effective as agents of democracy than the critics of the Soviet system would have us believe. I do know that they existed on the morrow of the Russian Revolution, and were the surest expression of its democratic soul.

These Soviets arose under stress of revolution because, amid the dissolution of the old despotic order, men had to find immediate means of standing together, and articulating their urgent common needs. There have been faint signs of the emergence from below of similar bodies among those who remain in districts of London and other blitzed cities sorely stricken by war. There have been improvisations in reception areas, where new problems of neighbourhood, such as billeting, have had to be faced. But the response has been small so far, because the bureaucracy has remained intact, and the political leaders of the new democracy from below have continued, on the whole, to collaborate with the bureaucracy, rather than work against it. A much greater dislocation than has yet occurred of the established machinery of administration would be needed to set the spirit of basic democracy ablaze among a people as used to being governed as ours. For our bureaucratic machine is on the whole quite competent at doing its job—competent and also honest. But it does not regard it as any part of its job to elicit the spirit of democracy. How could it, when the spirit of democracy is essentially untidy and unruly, whereas the bureaucrat lives by rules, forms and pigeon holes in which humanity, chopped up fine, can be neatly filed?

But, I hear the bureaucrats and their friends objecting— but it is altogether a fallacy to suppose that the ordinary man wants, either at his workplace or in the neighbourhood of his home, to be for ever talking politics. For proof he doesn't, go into the pubs and see. Go into the Women's Institutes, the Community Centres, listen in tubes and trains and restaurants. Go where you will, and hear for yourself. It isn't politics that interests the ordinary man. The nearest he gets to politics even under war conditions is air raids; and that isn't politics: it's sheer personal concern *plus* sporting interest.

Well, I know that. Most men and women aren't interested in politics because (*a*) they couldn't do anything much about them even if they were, given society as it now is; (*b*) politics aren't interesting usually, until you have already some very strong reason for being interested in them, and a tolerably clear notion of what they ought to be about; (*c*) the politicians, or most of them, don't want most people to be interested, except at election times, and don't do anything to get them continuously interested; (*d*) the bureaucrats want most people *not* to be interested, and will do their best to stamp out any organisation likely really to express the ordinary man's point of view; (*e*) the vested interests don't want ordinary people prying too closely into their various concerns; (*f*) it is simpler to govern a society when most people are not interested in its government, and no one quite knows whether the people, if it took to having a mind of its own, would agree with him or not. It is therefore safest to let sleeping dogs lie.

Need we wonder that ordinary men and women, under these conditions, are interested in politics only at rare moments when politics visibly and unmistakably comes and makes havoc of their lives? There has never been since the great days of Athens (save perhaps for a very brief while in Calvin's Geneva) a State, or even a city, whose rulers thought it part of every citizen's right and duty to take a continuous and active interest in political affairs.

I do not go so far as that. All I ask is that we should set out so to organise our new societies as to encourage every citizen to become politically conscious, and to believe in democracy as a precious possession of the people. And I assert that, in these days of huge States and huge-scale production, there is no way of doing this except by building up on a foundation of small neighbourhood groups, territorial and economic, because such groups alone have in them the essential qualities of unmediated, direct democracy based on personal contact and discussion, and on close mutual knowledge and community of small-scale, immediate problems. This only is democracy's sure foundation : given that, we can, I believe, safely raise upon it what towering sky-scrapers we please.

CHAPTER XV

THE SOCIALIST TASK

THIS BOOK has been a plea to my fellow-Socialists for three things. I have asked them, in thinking about the New Europe which we have to build, to think supra-nationally, to think democratically, and to think realistically. I have asked them to think supra-nationally, because none of the root problems can be solved on the plane of merely national thinking, or by mere association between a number of independent, sovereign States. War cannot be prevented so, or plenty be made the basis of the new order, or the reality of national freedom be secured. The new order has to be built on a huge scale, because hugeness is enforced on mankind by the technical progress that has been made in almost every art, except the art of living.

I have asked them to think democratically, because there is an evident danger that this need for huge-scale, supra-national organisation may submerge democracy. Men are being required to organise their common affairs over areas much larger than that of any single nation, before they have mastered the art of organising them on the smaller scale of the nation, or even the province. It is much easier to organise huge groupings from above than from below; and the line of least resistance in face of technical growth would be to let the Hitlers of the world organise it as they please, treading all democracy under their feet. This, fortunately, the traditions of freedom and independence which exist among men, most strongly in the most advanced societies, but also among not a few backward peoples, forbid mankind to do; and resistance to Hitler's attempts at forcible unification groups itself round the sentiment of nationality over a large part of Europe. Even in the Soviet Union, though the war is primarily one for the defence of Socialism, the spirit of nationality comes in, to reinforce the determination of the Soviet peoples.

This is to the good: for humanity needs against Nazism every reinforcement that it can find. Moreover, the spirit of nationality is in itself a fine thing, though it is easily perverted into notions of racial or imperial domination. National feeling is a creative expression of the human spirit, and Socialists have no need to be afraid of it. To say that "the workers have no country" would not mean, even if it correctly expressed their spirit, as it does not, that they ought to have none, but rather that they have been wrongfully dispossessed of the countries which should be theirs.

Yet nationality becomes a danger, if it gets in the way of the creation of units of government big enough to cope effectively with the problems of the modern world. As soon as the idea of nationality is identified with that of absolute State sovereignty—of the right of each nation to sovereign independence—it gets disastrously across the needs of our time. It is therefore indispensable that these two ideas shall be prised apart; and upon Socialists, as the chief exponents of an international gospel related to the modern world, falls the principal responsibility for bringing this about.

In order to bring it about, we must get into our heads a clear distinction between those common services which do need to be organised on a vast scale in order to make them effective, and those which do not. We must, moreover, set out with a determination to confine huge-scale organisation strictly to its proper sphere and, for every vast instrument we are compelled to set up, we must be at pains to create a counteragent by increasing the effectiveness of small-scale groupings. The more we need the supra-national State, the more we need to set over against it really democratic methods of administrations in our towns and villages, provinces and regions, and in the national areas of which the supra-national area is made up.

One great help in doing this is that, to the extent of our success in creating a supra-national authority powerful enough to keep society free from war and to set on foot a general system of planning for plenty, there is less to impel any particular group of men to desire largeness. Nations want to be big, in a world in which bigness seems to add to security. But if war has been outlawed and a fair sharing out of the world's resources of essential materials tolerably assured, there will be no strong reason for the men of any nation to continue to desire bigness for its own sake. If a particular nation is both numerous and fairly homogeneous, it will no doubt wish to be recognized as a large unit within the supra-national union of which its nationals are members. But, even so, it will probably tend to break itself up for purposes of administration into smaller units, within which there will be fuller opportunity for the practice of democratic self-government. And, where there exist within the frontiers of such a nation *enclaves* of different nationality, there will be no such reasons as there have been hitherto for resisting the demands of these groups for recognition, either as separate nations on their own, or at least as national minorities with a right to their own cultural autonomy and a right to form links with fellow-nationals from whom they are geographically divided. The establishment of supra-national States will clear the way for a multiplication of national groupings, on a basis, not of complete sovereign independence, but of cultural self-determination.

Thinking democratically implies a readiness, not merely to accept this sort of proliferation of national life, but positively to encourage it, up to the limits set by the need for common action over a supra-national area. For democracy means, in one of its aspects, the affording to men of the fullest possible opportunities to express what is in them in diverse ways; and one very important medium for such expression is that of the national group.

This, however, is of course nothing like the whole of democracy. It is only one of its essentials. Democracy involves also a recognition of the equality of individual human rights. The national spirit has hitherto all too often been made the prey of dominant classes, which have used it as a means of securing their own positions of privilege. Nationalist parties have become increasingly identified with social reaction, on the basis of attempts to represent old abuses as parts of the national tradition, and therefore untouchable without danger to the spirit of the nation.

This reactionary nationalism of privilege was emphatically not the nationalism which helped to inspire the French

Revolution; it was rather that of Burke and the aristocrats who fought with all their might against the new ideas. It is necessary to-day, when nationalism is bound to play a large part in the coming struggle for the liberation of Europe, to rid it of the reaction in which it has become enveloped, and to restore to it its revolutionary democratic character. The nationalism of the French Revolution, before Napoleon had perverted it into imperialism, was not a thing standing by itself, or exclusive to any particular country. It was an expression of the idea, applicable to all peoples, that the inhabitants who dwelt together in a country and felt a sense of community one with another as its citizens ought to possess that country and to direct its government for the common welfare. This idea did not, in those days, connote Socialism or public ownership; for Socialism had not yet arisen, except in purely Utopian forms. It connoted rather the appropriation of the land by the peasants, the abolition of feudal claims and overweening powers based on prescriptive right, and the opening of the gates of economic opportunity to every citizen. But Socialism is only the translation of these ideas into terms appropriate to a later epoch. It was possible to distribute a great estate among the peasants: it is not possible to distribute a railway or a power-station or a giant factory. If the people are to possess the vast instruments of modern production, the only possible way is for this possession to be in common to them all.

It is our task to recreate democratic nationalism in this, its Socialist form, as a demand for common ownership as the necessary basis of social equality. We must make the new national revolutions movements towards the acquisition for the whole people of economic as well as political power. And we must make it clear that this kind of nationalism does not set one nation against another, but makes all the democratic national movements partners in a common cause. That is why there is no antagonism between this democratic, Socialist nationalism and the struggle to build up the new society on a supra-national basis. The essential thing is that the peoples should possess their countries: whether they are to possess them severally or in common is a matter of administration and technical convenience— provided only that there is enough power and vitality in the smaller units of government to counteract the dangers of bureaucratic centralisation.

This vitality is no mere matter of the machinery of government, but depends on the entire society being permeated by a spirit of social equality. The national spirit will find for itself democratic expression, in both local and national affairs, in proportion as the people can regard themselves realistically as partners sharing the responsibility for the improvement of their common estate. But they will feel this, not merely because they are joint possessors of the nation's resources, but because they feel themselves equal to the task of using them. A sense of power and mastery, diffused among the general body of the people, is an indispensable ingredient of democracy.

This sense of mastery is closely connected with social equality. The sense of equality, above all else, gives the system of government in Russia its democratic character, despite very much that seems to us to be undemocratic in the working of its political institutions. As against this, the absence of equality, or the sense of it, largely destroys the democracy of the Western parliamentary countries, despite their formal acceptance of universal suffrage. The vote means much in a society of equals, much less where recognised social inequality contradicts its democratic pretensions.

But equality alone will not give the sense of mastery. For this there is required something more positive than a mere absence of class distinctions or gross disparities of wealth or status. Equality has to be conceived positively, as equal responsibility as well as the enjoyment of equal rights. It has to be regarded as carrying with it the obligation to be vigilant in its defence, and to play an active part in the conduct of affairs. Not that every citizen has to turn himself into a politician, save in the last resort for the defence of his and his fellows' rights. That is not necessary. A man can play his active rôle in industry or in social affairs, as well as in politics, in a society which regards these things also as matters of public service and concern.

Thus, in urging my fellow-Socialists to think democratically, I am urging them to think in terms of positive social equality, and not merely of the formal 'democracy' of the ballot-box. I am urging them to try to build up in Europe conditions which will give to the common men in all countries a sense of mastery and responsibility for upholding the new democratic system under which they are to live. This implies education for citizenship—active citizenship— but it implies more than that. For this masterful sense of social equality can be born in men only as a result of successful struggle, and only when the outcome of the struggle has been the destruction of the class-system.

Now, the danger of 'liberal' Social Democracy, with its acceptance of parliamentarism as its instrument, is that it is prone to overlook this very necessity of creating among its adherents a sense of power and of direct responsibility for the affairs of State. The voting system, taken by itself and used merely as an instrument of representation, encourages in men a belief that the responsibility for good government rests on their representatives, and not on themselves. It encourages slackness, listlessness, and therewith limpness in the hour of crisis. Nor is this irresponsibility of the represented compensated for by the development of finer qualities in the representatives. For they in turn slough off their responsibility for action by protesting that their duty is to do what the electors want, rather than to act courageously in the light of their own beliefs; and the result is apt to be seen in a general flabbiness of public spirit, and an attitude of cynical disbelief in the fundamentals of the democratic creed.

Neither leaders nor followers who have fallen into this mood are of much use in times of real crisis. They may jog on, well enough to all seeming, in quiet periods, when no great decisions have to be made; but the hour of trial will find them out. It found out the Italians, at the time of the March on Rome; the Germans, at the fall of the Weimar Republic; and the French, in the calamitous defeat of 1940. In a lesser degree it found out the British Labour Party in the crisis of 1931.

The lesson of these failures is that a party or a movement which professes democracy as its faith will go down to defeat unless it interprets democracy in an active sense. Passive democracy is a contradiction in terms: it means a democracy either merely formal, concealing undemocratic realities, or in decay, and incapable of effective self-defence.

Soviet democracy, as it has just shown by its rally in face of the Nazi menace, passes this test of activity, despite all its imperfections and errors of recent years. British democracy also showed its vitality in the great rally of the British people, and especially of the British workers, after the fall of France. But there is a difference. In the Soviet Union the workers can rally to the support of a State which is, in all essentials, their own. Here, they are compelled to ally themselves as still subordinate partners with a governing class which remains in possession of the key 'controls' of both industry and politics. They cannot feel that the discipline to which they submit for the sake of the war effort is self-imposed, or that the country they are gallantly defending is theirs in any full sense. This did not, as it might have done and as similar conditions largely did in France, paralyse their wills. They carried on in spite of it; and they are carrying on to-day. But they would have rallied more effectively, and the war effort would have been much more complete and well organised than it is, if they had not been in the position of defending a democratic aspiration, rather than a democratic reality. They rose to maintain their right to work for a better social system, and not to defend a system already in being which satisfied their democratic demands.

Nevertheless, what they fought for was worth defending; for in spite of all its undemocratic qualities it did embody for them large elements of real democracy. This democracy existed less in the machinery of government or the structure of the economic system than in a vigorous tradition of free association for a wide range of social ends. The real democracy of Great Britain was born largely in its dissenting chapels, spread thence to Trade Unionism, to the Co-operative movement, and to an immense variety of forms of voluntary private association for purposes of every sort and kind. The prevalence of this spirit of free association, and its embodiment in social tissue of many sorts, gave British democratic feeling a toughness in its hour of trial which was lacking in countries less permeated by the traditions of free speech and voluntary grouping.

This associative spirit is, indeed, the essential basis of British democracy. It is precisely the feature of the British system which admirers and imitators of the British parliamentary system are apt to miss. Without it the British Parliament would be a mere mockery of the democratic spirit, as many Parliaments set up in other countries without this complement have actually been. Representative government, in its parliamentary form, cannot be made to work democratically unless it rests upon firm foundations of civil liberty and freedom of organisation for voluntary groups.

Continental Socialists who profess Social Democratic, as against Communistic, doctrines must bear this truth in mind. Formal democracy of the parliamentary kind can become real only where the citizens, or large numbers of them, perform an active political rôle. The Soviet system, as it developed during the formative period of the Russian Revolution, was a way of organising this direct participation of large bodies of citizens in the responsibilities of government. It was the only way open, when this participation had to be improvised suddenly, amid the collapse of an autocratic régime which had used all means in its power of stamping out free speech and freedom to associate for common ends. The Soviet form of organisation may not be necessary for this purpose where free speech is an established tradition and voluntary associations have been able to flourish under a parliamentary régime. Parliaments may, under these conditions and with this backing, be able to play a constructive rôle in the hour of crisis. But wherever this social tissue of voluntary and free association does not exist, it will have to be improvised if democracy is to carry the day. Parliaments or Constituent Assemblies cannot by themselves supply the requisite constructive force. This force must come from the body of the people, organised for action; and when the people is not already so organised, the Soviet is the obvious instrument for organising it quickly, and setting it effectively to work.

The moral of this is that it is foolish, now, for Social Democrats to emphasise their differences from the Communists. For the Social Democrats cannot bring about revolutions in Europe, or hold them to Socialist courses, without invoking the instruments of Sovietism—that is, precisely the instruments which Communists will set out to create. The destruction of the Trade Unions, the Co-operative Societies, and the other forms of free association which used to exist in the countries which the Nazis have overrun, leaves a void; and this void can be filled in the hour of Nazi defeat only by improvisation. The Trade Unions and the Cooperative Societies cannot be rebuilt in a day or a week. Soviets can. That is the essential truth which continental Social Democrats have to be brought to understand.

Soviets will be, over all Nazi-occupied Europe, indispensable instruments of the coming revolution. But it does not follow that these Soviets must everywhere turn into instruments of totalitarian Socialism after the Russian

model. Far from it. Though the structure of free democratic
association cannot be rebuilt in a day, it can be rebuilt quite
quickly, where the tradition of it exists and is strong in the
minds of the people. The Soviets, in such countries, can
become the instruments of a new and reinvigorated parliamentarism, of a 'liberal' Socialism, and of a policy of tolerant
democracy: they need not involve the creation of a totalitarian régime. The great thing for Social Democrats is not
to be afraid of them—not to be afraid of the people whom
they aspire to lead. To be afraid of the people is, in truth,
the ultimate betrayal of democracy and of the Socialist
cause.

At the beginning of this chapter I urged my fellow-
Socialists to do three things: to think supra-nationally,
democratically—and realistically. This third thing, realism, is the hardest thing of all to learn. It so often involves
doing, not what one wants to do, not what one has planned
to do, not what, in an ultimate sense, one thinks the right
thing to do, but simply the best that can be done under the
circumstances. There is a danger here; for when a man has
decided that he cannot do what he wants, or has planned,
or thinks finally right, he is exceedingly apt to fall back on
taking the line of least resistance—which is the very antithesis of acting realistically. Political realism implies the
possession of high certainty about ends, which allows of great
elasticity about means. Therein it differs from opportunism,
which implies uncertainty about the ends themselves.

In relation to Socialism, the realist politician is he who,
having made up his mind completely that Socialism is his
objective, is thereafter prepared to work for Socialism by any
means which are not destructive of Socialist ends, and have
to be excluded on that ground. Socialism is not a mere
theory made out of air, but a vision of the right line of development for a civilisation which has already for centuries
been travelling a certain road. It is the culminating point in
a process of development which has already endowed

Western civilisation with certain possessions, including a certain ethic, of high human value. Any means which would have the effect of destroying, or of seriously undermining, these values are excluded by the very nature of the end which is being sought. To repudiate, in the name of Socialism, the ethic which alone can provide a foundation for the successful working of a Socialist society is a monstrous heresy. It can result only in poisoning the springs of the Socialist faith. Socialists cannot discard 'bourgeois morality': they have to build upon it, and give it a new and wider interpretation in the light of their belief in social equality and democracy as active agents of human progress.

Realism is not opportunism, but its very antithesis. The realist, holding fast to the achievements of civilisation, will use them as means to the achievement of his ends. So far from refusing to appeal to such feelings as social compunction or hatred of suffering or the sense of just dealing between man and man, he will make use of these appeals for all they are worth. And, in the advanced Western countries they are worth a great deal, though very possibly they were not worth much in Russia in 1917.

The realist will not be afraid of morality, or ready to dismiss it as a mere reflection of prevailing economic relationships. He will not only appeal to it, but accept it as his own guide and inspiration, trying at the same time to endow it with fuller content and more democratic meaning. The most disastrous mistake of the Communists in their efforts to convert the Western workers was their attempt to discard 'bourgeois morality' in favour of a hard-boiled, 'scientific' attitude. For the Western workers were not hard-boiled; and the hard boiling they received in the Communist Parties of the Western countries was as apt to convert them into Fascists as anything else. If there were no morality, but only science, why not? It could not be more 'moral' to be on one side rather than on the other.

Realism involves, then, accepting and seeking to develop

the established morality of Western civilisation. It involves building on the Christian ethic, though not necessarily accepting the Christian theology. It involves recognizing that men have ideals, and that only by enlisting their idealism can Socialism be made flesh. The Nazis, to be sure, have built their system by flouting the Christian ethic, and appealing from it to the barbarous appetites which exist in the underminds even of civilised men. But the Nazis have done this, and can do it with success, because they are not seeking to develop the values of Western civilisation to a higher point, but to destroy these values, and to revert to a way of living which has its roots in an un-civilised pagan past. Nazi immoralism is no model for the propagandists of Socialism to follow. If they attempt to follow it, they stultify their own efforts, and hand over their converts as helpless victims to the Nazi propaganda machine.

But realism does involve, besides this ethical fixity of conduct, an absence of dogmatism about means. It involves a readiness to work with better people against worse, and to take what can be got that is better than any practicable alternative. It involves a readiness to compromise, not with evil, but with imperfection; and it involves, above all else, keeping your eye all the time upon the ordinary man and his desires. For Socialism, when all is said and done, has value, not as a dogmatic system, but as an instrument for adding to the sum of human happiness. It is valuable only in proportion as men will be happier under it than under any alternative system under which it is really open to them to live.

This amounts, at the moment, to a plea for wide tolerance among Socialists, actual and potential, of different schools and ways of thought. The world is filled to-day with men and women who are not Socialists in any formal sense, but are acutely aware that their lives, and those of their friends and neighbours, are being spoilt by the utter insecurity of human affairs. They have passed through an epoch of peace between wars, and found it an epoch of empty mouths and idle hands vainly clamouring for hope. They have seen this desolate peace give place to a war which threatens to bring the entire structure of civilisation down in ruins. They want to know why they are so bandied about—so unwanted one day, so wanted the next for tasks which they loathe as immoral and foolish interruptions to the affair of living. These men and women are potential Socialists. They will become Socialists as fast as they become convinced that Socialism, and only Socialism, is able to put an end to all the meaningless flurry and insecurity. But they will not be converted by dogmas, but only by the demonstrated capacity of Socialists to ride the storm and tackle, better than other would-be rulers, the actual problems of our times.

This situation calls for a broad-minded, tolerant Socialism, capable of appealing to a wide diversity of men and women. Broadmindedness and tolerance do not mean weakness or want of determination, though these things are often confused. The weak of mind and will are oftentimes the most obstinate and the most dogmatic. The realist can afford to be tolerant and broad-minded, because he is certain of himself.

I appeal, then, to my fellow-Socialists to think supra-nationally, democratically, and realistically, and on this basis to get together here and now, British and Russians and exiles from all the occupied countries, to work out their plans for the construction of the new Europe on firm, Socialist foundations. I appeal to them for speed as well as courage, and for broad-mindedness as well as faith. For their business is not only to agree as Socialists but to make themselves the effective leaders of the peoples. But they cannot lead the peoples unless they follow the people's thoughts, and continually reshape their politics in the light of changing opportunities and changing attitudes among the common run of men. Socialism is not a dogma, but a movement, needing imaginative and coherent leadership. To study the facts and the people, and to make a policy which will enable the people to handle the facts effectively, in the pursuit of happiness—these are the essential tasks for those who aspire to lead poor stricken Europe out of its tribulations into the light of a new day.